100 WALKS IN
SCOTLAND

RENFREWSHIRE COUNCIL	
178699021	
Bertrams	21/03/2011
	£4.99
CEN	

Produced by AA Publishing
© AA Media Limited 2010

Published by AA Publishing (a trading name of AA Media Limited, whose registered office is Fanum House, Basing View, Basingstoke, Hampshire RG21 4EA; registered number 06112600)

 This product includes mapping data licensed from Ordnance Survey® with the permission of the Controller of Her Majesty's Stationery Office.
© Crown copyright 2010. All rights reserved. Licence number 100021153

ISBN: 978-0-7495-6499-5
A04143

These routes appear in the AA Local Walks series and *1001 Walks in Britain*.

theAA.com/shop
Printed in China by Leo Paper Group

Picture credits
All images are held in the Automobile Association's own photo library (AA World Travel Library) and were taken by the following photographers:
Front cover D Forss; 3 M Alexander; 6 S Anderson; 9 M Hamblin; 10 J Smith.

Opposite: Caerlaverock Castle, surrounded by a moat

Contents

SCOTLAND

Scotland

Almost half the size of England, yet with barely one fifth of its population, Scotland is a country of huge spaces and mountains on a grand scale. It is also a nation steeped in history and cultural diversity.

Scotland

Vast lochs penetrating to the heart of the mountains – this is how we perceive the Scottish identity, and yet it is only part of the story. In the east the border lands with their hilltops and deep valleys produce tales and people very different from the Celtic 'kilts' of the west. The southwest also has Celtic origins mixed up with ancient Britons, and with Irish and Viking traditions. The Southern Uplands form a barrier between the Scots and the English, and host some of the most colourful and bloody chapters in Scotland's history. To the east, the high, rounded Borders have harboured proud families. In late medieval times they were the reivers, striking into England to take cattle and pillage. The Union of the Crowns ended this lawlessness, but their balladry lived on – immortalised by Robert Burns, Sir Walter Scott and Hugh MacDiarmid.

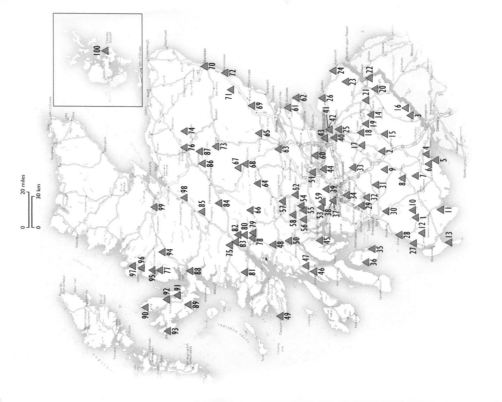

In the southwest religious conflict in the 17th century tore families apart and culminated in the 'killing times', when troops loyal to the Crown were set against Presbyterian worshippers and many hundreds died.

The central belt is where Scotland's Industrial Revolution set the country on course to become the engine of the British Empire. From the Clydeside yards came the ships that kept a maritime kingdom playing on a world stage. The rival cities of Edinburgh and Glasgow vie for supremacy. Glasgow has the people, the football teams and the architecture of Charles Rennie Macintosh; Edinburgh has the political and royal capitals, the festival and the tourists.

But it is the Highlands that have come to define Scotland. Barely have you left Glasgow's northern suburbs and their breathtaking panoramas come into view. It is no coincidence that Loch Lomond is at the heart of Scotland's first National Park. There are many differences in the Highland scene as you travel from west to east. The western mountains are jagged and rise up fiercely from the glens. In the east they are less spiky, but no less massive. On both sides of the A9 you'll

find deep valleys and lochs. The clear waters of the Spey Valley have long been famous for salmon fishing and as an ingredient in whisky.

The Southern Uplands

The size of the Southern Uplands always comes as a surprise. The scale of the Devil's Beeftub, near Moffat, will cause you to catch your breath. You will understand why the Tweed Valley commands so great a place in history when you follow this great river as it winds away from Peebles or Dryburgh. Other border towns have their own stories. Selkirk was the birthplace of the explorer Mungo Park. Mary, Queen of Scots came close to death while staying in a house near Jedburgh Abbey and at Traquair you'll find the oldest inhabited residence in Scotland. The Uplands continue into the southwest. The Nith Estuary and the Solway are guarded by the astonishing three-cornered stronghold of Caerlaverock Castle. Further west, Wigtown's notoriety stems from the execution by drowning of two Covenanter women in 1685.

Pages 6–7: Cruachan Dam and Loch Awe
Left: Braemar village in autumn

Industrial Origins

Looking back up the Nith Valley and its tributaries, the pretty village of Moniaive has long been attractive to artists and, in nearby Glenkiln, you'll find a whole valley dedicated to sculpture. The iron foundries at Dunaskin were created because of the abundance of raw materials in the area, and today you can visit the visitor centre and walk among the ruins of the deserted workers' village. At the industrial site of New Lanark, Robert Owen's planned mill town is now a World Heritage Site.

Heart of the Nation

Several places claim to be the heart of Scotland, but Edinburgh is among the most worthy. This city commands several walks – up to its castle and around its Georgian New Town. Edinburgh's backcloth is formed by the Pentland Hills, an odd corner of mountain rising from an upland plateau. Hidden on its northern flank is Rosslyn Glen, with its chapel and castle. Before you are done with the south, visit St Abb's Head, then head across the Forth to Culross and St Andrews. Visit the amazing Falkirk Wheel, joining the Forth and Clyde Canal with the Union Canal, and making east–west navigation possible again. The Kilsyth tow path on the Forth and Clyde can be combined with a return along the Antonine Wall.

Highland Vision

From the Byne Hill in Ayrshire, Ailsa Craig stands prominently in the Firth of Clyde. Here, you can glimpse the Highlands as the peaks of Arran rise from the sea. Another ferry will take you to the Cowal Peninsula, where Puck's Glen is a lovely corner of the former Benmore Estate with an important botanic garden. Glasgow folk flocked to such semi-wild sites and found resorts and refuges at places such as Carbeth, Aberfoyle and Loch Katrine.

The Highlands offer some of the best walking in Britain – to the Hidden Valley of Glen Coe, beneath the slopes of Ben Nevis and on Skye, where the weirdly shaped Quiraing is fascinating to explore. Little Raasay will give an island experience all by itself, and Portree makes a fine base for a gentle walk with fine views.

Mull, too, is worth crossing to, even if just to hop over to Iona, where Scottish kings were laid to rest. It rivals Kilmartin Glen in importance in Scottish history, but cannot claim the crowning stones of Dunadd.

To the East

This is the home of the Scots pine and the Rothiemurchus woodlands. You'll find royal stories and whisky to pursue at Braemar and Glenlivet. At the mouth of Glen Tilt stands Blair Athol, where the Duke raised his own army, while Glen Prosen opens out to Kirriemuir, the birthplace of J M Barrie. And Stirling spans the gap between Highland and Lowland.

Using this Book

❶ Information panels

Information panels show the total distance and total amount of ascent (that is the accumulated height you will ascend throughout the walk). An indication of the gradient you will encounter is shown by the rating 0–3. Zero indicates fairly flat ground and 3 indicates undulating terrain with several very steep slopes.

❷ Minimum time

The minimum time suggested is for approximate guidance only. It assumes reasonably fit walkers and doesn't allow for stops.

❸ Start points

The start of each walk is given as a six-figure grid reference prefixed by two letters indicating which 100km square of the National Grid it refers to. You'll find more information on grid references on most Ordnance Survey maps.

❹ Abbreviations

Walk directions use these abbreviations:

L – left
L–H – left-hand
R – right
R–H – right-hand
**Names which appear on signposts
are given in brackets, for example
('Bantam Beach').**

❺ Suggested maps

Details of appropriate maps are given for each walk, and usually refer to 1:25,000 scale Ordnance Survey Explorer maps. We strongly recommend that you always take the appropriate OS map with you. The maps in this book are there to give you the route and do not show all the details or relief that you will need to navigate around the routes provided in this collection. You can purchase Ordnance Survey Explorer maps at all good bookshops.

❻ Car parking

Many of the car parks suggested are public, but occasionally you may find you have to park on

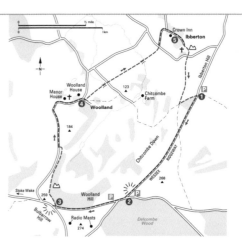

❶ ❷ ❺ ❸ ❻

LOCATION Walk title
From the tops of Bulbarrow Hill to the valley floor and back, via an atmospheric church.

4.25 miles/6.8km 2hrs **Ascent** 591ft/180m **⚠ Difficulty** ☐
Paths Quiet roads, muddy bridleways, field paths, 2 stiles
Map OS Explorer 117 Cerne Abbas & Bere Regis **Grid ref** ST 791071
Parking Car park at Ibberton Hill picnic site

County • REGION

❶ Turn **L** along road, following Wessex Ridgeway, with Ibberton laid out below to **R**. Road climbs gradually, and you see masts on Bulbarrow Hill ahead.
❷ After 1 mile (1.6km) pass car park on **L**, with plaque about Thomas Hardy. At junction bear **R** and immediately **R** again, signposted 'Stoke Wake'. Pass another car park on **R**. Woods of Woolland Hill now fall away steeply on **R**. Pass radio masts to **L** and reach small gate into field on **R**, near end of wood. Before taking it, go extra few steps to road junction ahead for wonderful view of escarpment stretching away west.
❸ Go through gate and follow uneven bridleway down. Glimpse spring-fed lake through trees on **R**. At bottom of field, path swings **L** to gate. Go through, on to road. Turn **R**, continuing downhill. Follow road into Woolland, passing Manor House and Old Schoolhouse, on **L** and **R** respectively.
❹ Beyond entrance, on **L**, to Woolland House turn **R** into lane and immediately **L** through kissing

gate. Path immediately forks. Take **L-H** track, down through marshy patches and young sycamores. Posts with yellow footpath waymarkers lead straight across meadow, with gorse-clad Chitcombe Down up **R**. Cross footbridge over stream. Go straight on to cross road. Keeping straight on, go through hedge gap. Bear **L** down field, cross stile and continue down. Cross footbridge and stile to continue along **L** side of next field. Go through gate to road junction. Walk straight up road ahead and follow it **R**, into Ibberton. Bear **R**.
❺ Continue up this road through village. This steepens and becomes path, bearing **R**. Steps lead up to church. Continue up steep path. Cross road and go straight ahead through gate. Keep straight on along fence, climbing steadily. Cross under power lines, continue in same direction, climbing steadily. Carry on open pasture to small gate in hedge. Do not go through gate, but turn sharp **L**, up slope, to small gate opposite car park.

112

the roadside or in a lay-by. Please be considerate when you leave your car, ensuring that access roads or gates are not blocked and that other vehicles can pass safely. Remember that pub car

parks are private and should not be used unless you are visiting the pub or you have the landlord's permission to park there.

Opposite: Dry-stone wall near Braemar, Cairngorms National Park

GLENTROOL The Battle Of Independence

Forest trails lead to a famous battlefield.

5 miles/8km 2hrs **Ascent** 300ft/91m ⚠ **Difficulty** ☐1

Paths Forest trails, metalled roads, 1 stile

Map OS Explorer 318 Galloway Forest Park North **Grid ref** NX 396791

Parking Caldons

1 Leave car park and follow Southern Upland Way markers. Cross bridge over Water of Trool. Cross another bridge over Caldons Burn. Next, take **L** on to footpath that runs along banks of river. Cross over bridge.

2 Follow this well waymarked trail and at fork by waymarker turn **R**, and then head uphill and into forest.

3 Keep on path uphill and through clearing, then go through kissing gate and re-enter woodland. Continue along southern side of Loch Trool until you reach interpretation board near the loch end. This marks the spot where Robert the Bruce and his army cleverly lured the superior English forces into a well-planned ambush and routed them.

4 Follow path from here, leaving woodland and heading downhill and to **L**, before leaving the Southern Upland Way. Turn **L**, go through two gates and over wooden bridge. Cross bridge over Gairland Burn and continue. Eventually reaching bridge

over Buchan Burn, cross over and take the path **L**, branching off uphill.

5 Follow this to top and Bruce's Stone, which was raised to commemorate the victory at the Battle of Glentrool, the first victory in the Independence Wars. From here, looking across the clear waters of the loch to the tree-clad hills opposite, is one of the finest views in Scotland. Follow track past stone then turn L on to narrow road. Head through car park and keep going until you reach waymarker on **L** which leads to forest trail, and take this to return to the start of the walk.

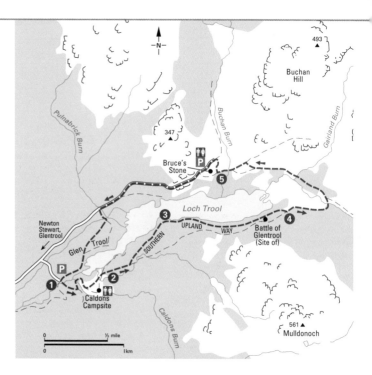

DEVIL'S BEEF TUB A Hearty Walk
Around Devil's Beef Tub near Moffat.

4.5 miles/7.2km 2hrs **Ascent** 1,076ft/328m ⚠ **Difficulty** ③
Paths Farm tracks, small paths; narrow path across steep Beef Tub slope
Map OS Explorer 330 Moffat & St Mary's Loch **Grid ref** NT 057128
Parking Lay-by just south of forest gateway
WARNING Bull with cows occasionally at Point ④

❶ Walk up A701 to forest gateway on **R**. Go through wooden gate on **R-H** side, to small path to **L** of fence. Climb rails at fence end, and ascend Annanhead Hill, keeping to **R** of plantation to summit trig point.

❷ Continue around flank of Peat Knowe, keeping wall and fence to your **L**. Follow path down Annanhead Hill, keeping to head of gully, where path meets wall. Walk to other side of gully.

❸ Past gully head, turn **R** on small path running above and **L** of grassy gully. As slope drops away, the path (Strait Step) bends **L** and contours on level line across steep slope, below craggy outcrops. As slope eases, path slants through bracken, heading to Coreknowe plantation. Just before plantation, you reach metal gate into field.

❹ If bull is grazing in field, pass above field and climb awkward fence into plantation. Slant down **R**, under trees, to gate into field with tiny footbridge. Otherwise, go through grey gate and down beside grassy bank.

Turn **L** on rough track to bottom corner of plantation. Track reaches gate above red-brick house. Through gate, signed 'Moffat', head into field to tiny footbridge, then bear **R** to pass **L** of white buildings of Corehead farm. Fence on **R** leads to gate on to farm's access track.

❺ Follow farm road along valley bottom.

❻ After cattle grid, at start of buildings, turn up **R** through gate signed 'footpath'. Stony track leads past house and through gate. Turn **R**, following track above stone wall. Eventually reach A701. Cross – take care – on to rough track opposite.

❼ Continue over Ericstane Hill. Bear **R** and follow track north round far side of hill. Track may be indistinct, ruts hidden under rushes. Pass through slight col to **L** of summit, to rejoin A701. Turn **R** to visit Covenanter memorial, or turn **L** to return to start.

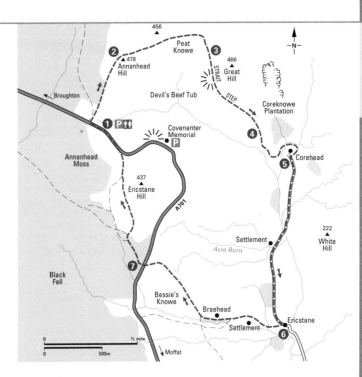

3

LANGHOLM A Poet's Passions

An exhilarating climb is followed by a gentle stroll past Hugh MacDiarmid's memorial.

3.75 miles/6km 2hrs **Ascent** 919ft/280m ⚠ **Difficulty** 2
Paths Firm hill paths and tarmac roads
Map OS Explorer 323 Eskdale & Castle O'er Forest **Grid ref** NY 364849
Parking Riverside car park (free)

❶ Cross grass downstream, then go through a hedge gap on **L** to pass through a small garden to the A7 above. Head into Langholm along High Street to post office on **L**.

❷ Immediately past post office, turn **L** up Kirk Wynd. It becomes tarred, then rough track running up to **L** of golf course to gate. Follow grassy path up and slightly **R** to reach green seat beside the natural spring, Whita Well.

❸ Now take path to **L** of seat, running steeply up hill. Follow it under line of pylons and up to top of Whita Hill. There are stone steps up to the monument, a 100ft (30m) high obelisk commemorating Sir John Malcolm, famous soldier, diplomat and scholar.

❹ From St John Malcolm's monument, walk back a few paces to join wide gravel track that runs in front of it, then turn **R**. It's easy walking now, following this clear track downhill. Eventually you reach unusual metal sculpture on **L-H** side. The sculpture, which resembles an open book, was created by Jake Harvey

and is a memorial to Hugh MacDiarmid.

❺ Bear **L** past sculpture to small car park, and turn **L**. You now simply follow road as it winds downhill – it's quite a long stretch but fairly quiet. Go back under line of pylons then, just after copse on your **R-H** side, take the path on **L**, signposted 'Langholm Walks 10'.

❻ Follow this footpath, slightly uphill and then above a wall, where it runs through small boggy patch. After this you shortly return to the gate you reached on your outward journey. Turn **R**, through gate, and retrace your outward route.

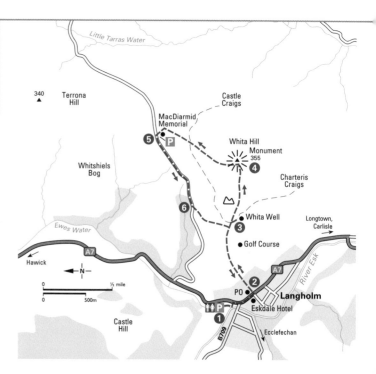

CAERLAVEROCK The Solway Merses

An ancient fortress and a nature reserve.

5.25 miles/8.4km 2hrs 30min **Ascent** 82ft/25m ⚠ **Difficulty** 1

Paths Country lanes, farm tracks and salt marsh, 1 stile

Map OS Explorer 314 Solway Firth **Grid ref** NY 051656

Parking Car park at Wildfowl and Wetlands Trust Reserve

❶ Exit car park and turn **R** on to farm road. Continue past farms of Newfield and Midtown then turn **L** and go past bungalow and houses. Just before farm of Hollands waymarker points to car park on **R**, and ahead for walks. Go ahead to farm steading, then turn **L**.

❷ Go through gate and on to farm track, which has high hedges on both sides. Continue along this track and on, across overgrown section, to end then turn **R** at signpost for Caerlaverock.

❸ Sign here informs that regulated wildfowling (shooting) takes place between 1 September and 20 February. Follow rough track through grass along merse edge in direction of arrow on footpath waymarker post. Path can be very boggy at all times and grass is high in summer.

❹ Path through nature reserve varies from faint to non-existent; Wellington boots are recommended. It splits at several points and meanders back and forth, but all lines of path rejoin.

❺ Eventually some cottages can be seen in field to **R**. Bear **R**, through gate and into field. Walk to **L** around field perimeter, past some cottages, then turn **L** through gate to emerge on to farm track, passing sign for Caerlaverock Castle and into castle grounds.

❻ Follow road past old castle, which has been excavated and has information, and go through wood with nature trail information boards to Caerlaverock Castle. There are children's playground, siege machine and picnic tables around castle.

❼ At far end go through arch and continue to T-junction with country lane. Turn **R** and continue for about 1 mile (1.6km), then turn **R** on to another lane signposted 'Wildfowl and Wetlands Reserve'. Continue on this road past farms of Northpark, Newmains and Nethertown and then back to start.

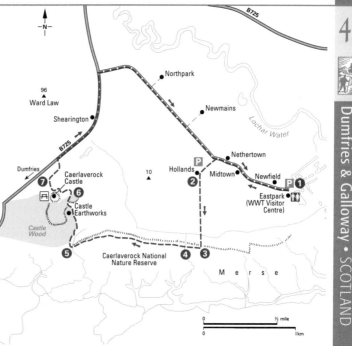

CARSETHORN The Solway Shore

Visit the birthplace of the 'father of the American Navy'.

5.5 miles/8.8km 2hrs 30min **Ascent** 82ft/25m ⚠ **Difficulty** ☐1

Paths Rocky seashore, woodland tracks and country road
Map OS Explorer 313 Dumfries & Dalbeattie, New Abbey **Grid ref** NX 993598
Parking Car park by beach at Carsethorn

❶ From car park at Carsethorn head down on to beach and turn **R**. Continue along shore for about 2 miles (3.2km). Beach here is sandy and may be strewn with driftwood, but if tide is in you will walk over more rocky ground.

❷ After reaching The House on the Shore, beside beach on your **R**, continue around headland and along beach to next one, then look for a faint path uphill to join well-defined track alongside stone wall.

❸ Continue along track and descend steeply to arrive at beach beside natural rock arch called Thirl Stane. You can go through arch to sea if tide is in, although if tide is out, sea will be in distance.

❹ Continue along rocks on pebble shore and up grassy bank to a car park. Exit car park on to lane. Continue on lane past Powillimount. Turn **R** when you get to lodge house on **R**-H side and walk along estate road to cottage birthplace of John Paul Jones and small museum.

❺ Continue along road past gates to Arbigland, on to road signed 'No vehicular traffic'. Follow road **R** and alongside some Arbigland Estate buildings.

❻ When road turns **L** at cottage, go **R** on dirt track. Follow track until it emerges on to surfaced road next to Tallowquhairn to **R**. Take road away from farm, turning sharply **L** around houses, then **R** and continue to T-junction.

❼ Turn **R** and follow road to **L**. Follow long road until **R** turn to South Carse. Go along farm road and through farm steading as far as possible, then turn **L**.

❽ To return to shore, walk along footpath passing brightly coloured caravan and to rear of cottages. Look out for narrow track heading down **R**, giving access to beach. Turn **L** along beach to car park.

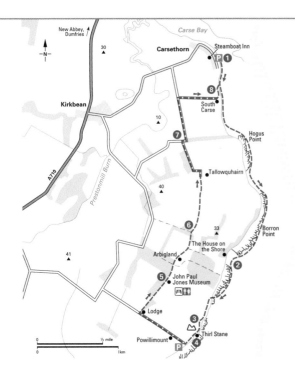

NEW ABBEY To Criffel

The 13th-century love story of the Lady Devorgilla, set forever in stone.

3.75 miles/6km 3hrs **Ascent** 1,686ft/514m ⚠ **Difficulty** ③
Paths Forest road, rough hill and wood tracks, 1 stile
Map OS Explorer 313 Dumfries & Dalbeattie **Grid ref** NX 971634
Parking Car park at Ardwall farm

❶ Exit car park via kissing gate, cross farm road and then go through another kissing gate and continue along track. Turn **R** after 70yds (64m) then head towards hill on track between dry-stone walls. When road starts to curve **L**, in front of wood, take rough track off to **R**.

❷ Follow track uphill through trees following by Craigrockall Burn. It narrows in places and ground is very uneven with several large boulders to climb over or around.

❸ At T-junction with forest road, keep straight ahead to pick up trail on other side and continue uphill. Cross another forest road and eventually reach a fence. Cross fence and veer to **L**, heading towards summit of Criffel.

❹ From trig point you'll have a superb view. Across the Solway to the south is England and hills of the Lake District. A little to the **R** of that is the Isle of Man, while Ireland's coast is visible to the west. The ancient Scotti tribe came from Ireland and founded Scotland.

On a good day the summit of Criffel is ideal for a picnic. When you've eaten your picnic and enjoyed the view head roughly north-west from cairn, following a faint path that leads towards broad ridge that runs from Criffel to neighbouring hill of Knockendoch. Head downhill, then continue, ascending again, to summit of Knockendoch.

❺ From summit cairn head east and go downhill. In summer, when the heather is particularly thick, the going can be fairly tough and you'll have to proceed slowly and with caution. Make for fence that runs across hill in front of you. Turn **R** here and follow it back to point you crossed on way up, then and retrace your steps to bottom of hill.

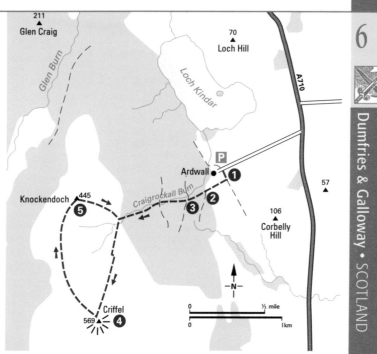

GLENKILN Outdoor Sculptures
Discover works of art in this unique countryside setting.

4 miles/6.4km 2hrs 30min **Ascent** 312ft/95m ⚠ **Difficulty** [2]
Paths Country roads, farm tracks, open hillside
Map OS Explorer 321 Nithsdale & Dumfries **Grid ref** NX 839784
Parking Car park in front of statue of John the Baptist

❶ From car park in front of John the Baptist statue return to main road and turn **R**. Cross cattle grid, turn **R**; go past statue to Marglolly Burn. Turn **L** and walk along bank towards Cornlee Bridge. Just before bridge turn **L** and head back to road. Henry Moore's Standing Figure is before you at junction with farm road.

❷ Turn **L** and head back on main road. Before entrance to Margreig farm on **R** is muddy track across field to gate in dry-stone wall. Head up and through gate then keep ahead, towards telephone pole. At pole veer **L** and follow track uphill. Glenkiln Cross should be visible before you.

❸ Take track closest to large tree in front of you. Cross over burn at tree and take path skirting to **L** of it. Veer **R** and head for high ground. When cross comes into view again head towards it.

❹ From cross turn to face Glenkiln Reservoir and head downhill towards telephone pole. Go through gate in fence at bottom of hill and turn **R** on to road. After short distance farm track leads uphill to **R**. Go

through gate and on to it. To **R** is Henry Moore's King and Queen.

❺ Continue on track. Go through gate, pass wooded area on **R** and then bare hillside until you spot stand of Scots pine on **L**. Leave road here and continue to trees and Epstein's Visitation. Return to road and continue to end to go through gate, cross over bridge then turn **L** on road.

❻ Go downhill on this road for 0.5 mile (800m), crossing cattle grid. Just before end of conifer plantation on **L**, look out for Moore's Two Piece Reclining Figure No.1 on **R**. Follow road downhill, turn **L** at junction and continue on this road to car park.

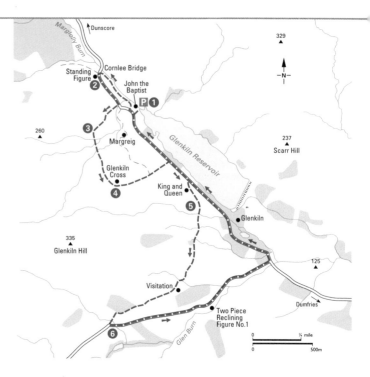

MONIAIVE The Glasgow Boys

The village that inspired the Glasgow Boys.

5 miles/8km 3hrs **Ascent** 295ft/90m ⚠ **Difficulty** 2
Paths Dirt roads, hill tracks, forest road and country lane
Map OS Explorers 321 Nithsdale & Dumfries, Thornhill; 328 Sanquhar & New Cumnock, Muirkirk
Grid ref NX 780910 (on Explorer 328) **Parking** Moniaive village car park

1 Exit car park and turn **R**. At nearby T-junction turn **R** and cross pedestrian bridge, beside garage, to enter Moniaive High Street at George Hotel. Walk along High Street to Market Cross of Moniaive, pass it, then turn **L** and cross road. Turn **R** at other side and head up Ayr Street, passing public toilets.

2 The imposing building on **R** with the clock tower is the former schoolmaster's house. Continue up Ayr Street passing park on **R** and wooden garages on **L**. Take next **R** on to narrow lane. Continue to end of lane and, at T-junction turn **R**.

3 Pass modern bungalow on **L**, then field, then turn **L** on to dirt road at end of field. Cross bridge and continue up road to Bardennoch. When the road curves **R** to enter grounds of house, go straight on and follow road, which goes up side of wood and uphill.

4 At end of woodland section go through a gate and continue uphill on road. Cross fence and at top, near ruin of Upper Bardennoch, go through another gate. From here continue to climb towards stand of

Scots pine, circle, keeping them on **R**, and continue to summit of Bardennoch Hill.

5 From summit continue towards woodland (wall running alongside to **R**). Head slightly downhill to corner where this wall meets one running in front of woodland. Cross wall and go on to a forest road.

6 Turn **R** and follow road downhill through several gates until it goes through final gate, at T-junction with country lane, where you turn **R**. At next T-junction **L** turn will take you to hamlet of Tynron, which is worth visiting. Otherwise turn **R** again.

7 Follow road past Dalmakerran farm, then uphill and through wood. Continue uphill passing cottage on **R** then, further along, another house. Road starts to go downhill again on to Dunreggan Brae. At bottom of hill re-enter Moniaive and turn **R** into car park.

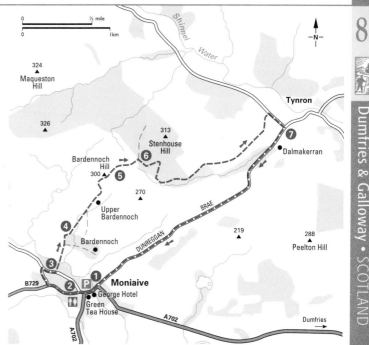

WANLOCKHEAD Scotland's Highest Village
Discover the secrets of lead and gold mining.

3.75 miles/6km 3hrs **Ascent** 525ft/160m ⚠ **Difficulty** 2
Paths Footpaths, hill tracks, hillside and old railway lines, 1 stile
Map OS Explorer 329 Lowther Hills, Sanquhar & Leadhills **Grid ref** NX 873129
Parking Museum of Lead Mining car park

1 With museum to your back turn **L** and join Southern Upland Way. Head uphill on steps then, at top, cross to stone building with large white door. Turn **R** on to a rough road, cross main road and take public footpath to Enterkine Pass. Follow this to front of white house.

2 Turn **L** on to course of old railway line. Follow this, cross road then go through long cutting to reach fence. Go over stile to get to Glengonnar Station then follow narrow path that runs along **L** side of railway tracks from here. Eventually path runs on to rough road and in distance see 2 terraced houses.

3 Where telephone wires intersect road, turn **L** at pole on the **L-H** side and follow fence line down to some sheep pens. Turn **R** at end of pens and walk to main road.

4 Turn **R** then almost immediately **L** on to hill road. Walk uphill on this until road bears sharp **R** and a dirt track forks off **L**. Turn **L** on to track and keep on it to gate. Cross over, then veer **L** on to faint track. Follow

track downhill to point where it comes close to corner of fence on **L**.

5 Cross fence and go ahead on very faint track through heather. Eventually, as track begins to look more like a path, reach a fork. Go **R** here and cross flank of hill passing through disused tips.

6 Path at this point is little more than series of sheep tracks and may disappear altogether but don't worry. Ahead is large conical spoil heap and, provided you keep heading towards it, you know you will be going in the **R** direction.

7 Towards end of hill track heads **L**, starts to make its way downhill, then passes behind row of cottages. Veer **R**, downhill, after cottages to join road. Turn **L** and continue past Glencrieff cottages, then turn **R**, leaving road and heading downhill again. Cross bridge and climb up on to Southern Upland Way. Turn **L** along it and follow this back to car park.

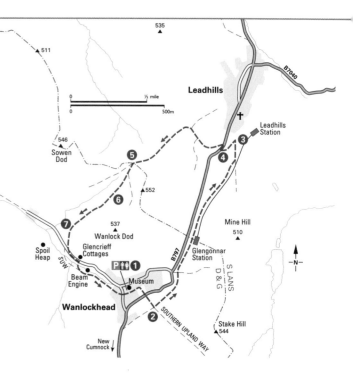

LOCH ENOCH Cycling On The Merrick
Follow in the cycle tracks of Davie Bell.

9 miles/14.5km 5hrs **Ascent** 2,339ft/713m ⚠ **Difficulty** ③
Paths Hill tracks, section to Loch Enoch can be very boggy, 1 stile
Map OS Explorer 318 Galloway Forest North **Grid ref** NX 415804
Parking Bruce's Stone car park

❶ From car park at Bruce's Stone head east along narrow road, across Buchan Bridge. Continue short distance then turn **L** and go uphill to cross stile. Follow path along wall, then veer **R** and head uphill to rejoin wall. Go through gate and turn **R** on to path. Follow this up valley of Gairland Burn with Buchan Hill on **L**.
❷ To **L** is ridge of Buchan Hill and to **R** is White Brae, and to far side of that Rig of the Jarkness. Do not cross Gairland but keep going on the path to reach Loch Valley, skirting it to west and then continue beside Mid Burn to reach Loch Neldricken.
❸ Head for far west corner of loch to find infamous Murder Hole featured by S R Crockett in *The Raiders* (1894). The story is based on a local legend that unwary travellers were robbed on these hills and their bodies disposed of in the loch.
❹ From Murder Hole head north, crossing burn and then wall. Pass to west of Ewe Rig and tiny Loch Arron and eventually reach south side of Loch Enoch. Don't worry if track vanishes or becomes indistinct, just keep

heading north to eventually reach loch.
❺ As you approach Loch Enoch you see outline of Mullwarchar beyond it and to **R**. When you reach loch go **L** and cross another wall. The slope in front of you is Redstone Rig and although you have 1,000ft (305m) to climb it is not particularly taxing.
❻ From summit cairn of Merrick head downhill towards narrow ridge called the Neive of the Spit to reach summit of Benyellary, Hill of the Eagle. From here follow footpath downhill beside a dry-stone wall then turn **L** and keep going downhill, into the forest, to reach bothy at Culsharg. From there continue downhill to return to car park.

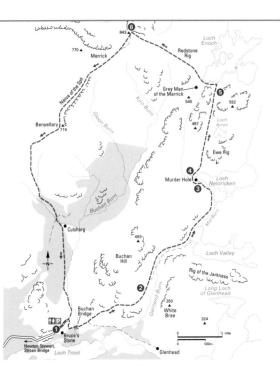

WIGTOWN The Killing Times

Visit the memorial to two women drowned at the stake for their religion.

4 miles/6.4km 3hrs **Ascent** 98ft/30m ⚠ **Difficulty** ☐1

Paths Roads, old railway tracks and pavements

Map OS Explorer 311 Wigtown, Whithorn & The Machars **Grid ref** NX 439547

Parking At Wigtown harbour

❶ Leave car park, turn **R** and head uphill on narrow country lane (Harbour Road). The house on **L** near top of road was station house for Wigtown. Before it is farm gate on **L**. Go through and on to farm track.

❷ Follow track to where it goes through another gate then veer **R** and climb up old railway embankment – good grassy surface. Proceed along length of embankment.

❸ Wall across track will stop you at point where former railway bridge carried track across River Bladnoch. Turn **R** and go down side of embankment and cross gate into field. Veer **R** and head across field to far corner then go through gate on to main road.

❹ Turn **L** and walk through Bladnoch. At junction by roundabout, cross road to enter Bladnoch Distillery car park. Visit distillery then head out of car park and turn **L** at roundabout. Continue along road (B7005) for 1 mile (1.6km) until you reach crossroads.

❺ Turn **R** on to B733, walk to Wigtown. At town centre bear L round square and head towards large and impressive former county buildings. Pass them on **R**, then church and war memorial on **L** and continue downhill. Eventually turn **R** into car park for Martyrs' Memorial.

❻ Walk through car park and then turn **R** and head along path leading to Martyrs' Memorial. Turn **L** and walk out over sands on a specially constructed wooden causeway to reach poignant memorial erected on spot where two women were drowned.

❼ Return to path and turn **L**. Go through kissing gate then another gate, slightly below level you are walking on and to **L**. At end of path go through another gate in front of station house, turn **L** on to Harbour Road and return to car park.

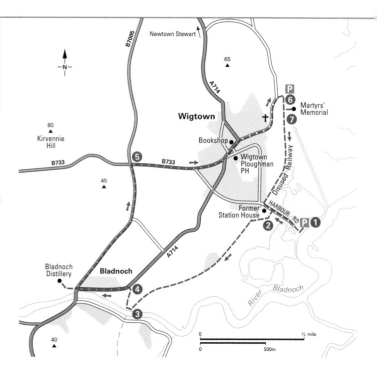

WELLS OF THE REES Ancient Stone Domes
A tough walk on the Southern Upland Way.

6.25 miles/10.1km 3hrs 30min **Ascent** 558ft/170m ⚠ **Difficulty** 3
Paths Forest roads, forest track, very rough ground
Map OS Explorer 310 Glenluce & Kirkcowan **Grid ref** NX 260735
Parking Near Derry farm

1 Cross cattle grid and head west along Southern Upland Way (SUW) on well-surfaced forest road. Pass Loch Derry, on **R** in just under 1 mile (1.6km) and then continue on forest road, passing signpost on **L** to Linn's Tomb.

2 Follow road as it curves to **R**, then, following SUW markerpost, turn **L**, leave road and head uphill. It's a steep climb from here, on well-trodden path with waymarkers.

3 Cross over forest road and then continue on uphill path heading towards summit of Craig Airie Fell. Reach summit at trig point.

4 From OS triangulation pillar, continue on well-marked path towards waymarker on horizon. Turn **L** at waymarker and head downhill on footpath that twists and turns to another waymarker near bottom. Turn **R** here and continue to edge of forest.

5 SUW now follows forest ride. Shortly arrive at clearing with cairn on **L**. Keep straight ahead following waymarkers to next clearing where sign points **L**

to Wells of the Rees. Turn **L** and head downhill, across dry-stone wall and then gap in another wall. In summer it is more difficult to find wells when the bracken is thick. First 2 wells are on **R** as you come through gap and other is to **L**.

6 Retrace steps from here to signpost and turn **L**. Continue along Southern Upland Way to reach junction with forest road. Turn **L** and follow it to end, then continue along faint path, cross wall and continue east towards Craigmoddie Fell.

7 Climb to highest point then look to **L** to Loch Derry then, to **R** of it, Derry farm. Head in a straight line for Derry farm then drop down off fell and pick up path heading towards Loch Derry. Follow this to go through a gate and on to the forest road. Turn **R** and return to Derry farm and car.

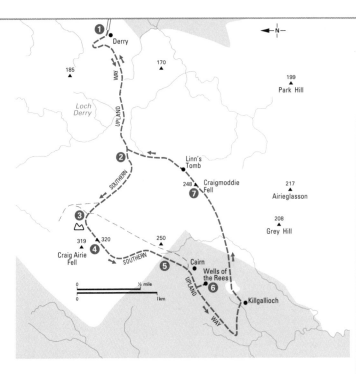

PORT LOGAN Fictional Ronansay

A walk around a picturesque fishing village where everything is not as it seems.

2.5 miles/4km 2hrs **Ascent** 492ft/150m ⚠ **Difficulty** 1
Paths Shoreline, country lanes and hill tracks, 1 stile
Map OS Explorer 309 Stranraer & The Rhins **Grid ref** NX 097411
Parking Public car park on road to Logan Fish Pond

❶ From car park go across wooden walkway, down some steps on to sand and turn **L** to walk along beach. When you reach start of village, climb on to road in front of Port Logan Inn. Turn **R** and then continue walking along main street, passing war memorial to reach village hall. In Two Thousand Acres of Sky the village hall featured as the village school, and had a school sign fixed to the front. There was also a timetable for Caledonian MacBrayne ferries displayed on a notice board on the wall. Opposite the village hall is a small but picturesque harbour with a rather unusual lighthouse. Nowadays, Port Logan harbour is used only by a few pleasure craft.

❷ Port Logan was a thriving fishing port in the past and during the filming of the television series, the pier was festooned with fishing gear, gas bottles and sacks of coal, but they were just props. Move away from harbour area and continue along road to farm of Muldaddie.

❸ Just before farm turn **L** on to old hill track and head uphill. Near the top look back downhill for a magnificent view back to the village and across Port Logan Bay to the Mull of Logan. Track is heavily overgrown here, and is blocked by barrier made from gates, but this can easily be crossed by going over stile at side.

❹ Continue along track to T-junction, following public footpath sign.

❺ Retrace your steps to Port Logan then go back on to beach, turn **R** and retrace your steps to car park. From here you can continue along rough road to Logan Fish Pond. It's **R** at end on **L** and is by only building there.

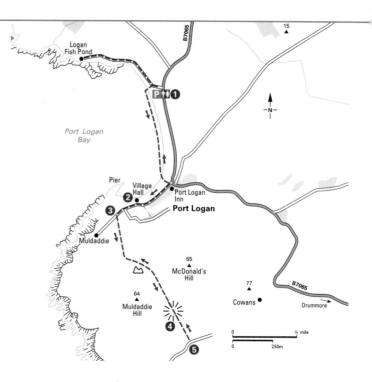

SELKIRK To The Wilds Of Africa

A gentle walk by Ettrick Water, laced with memories of the great explorer Mungo Park.

4 miles/6.4km 1hr 40min **Ascent** 131ft/40m ⚠ **Difficulty** ①
Paths Riverside paths and woodland tracks, town streets, 4 stiles
Map OS Explorer 338 Galashiels, Selkirk & Montrose **Grid ref** NT 469286
Parking West Port car park in Selkirk

❶ From Park's statue, walk to Market Place, go **R** down Ettrick Terrace, **L** at church, then sharp **R** on Forest Road. Continue downhill, cutting off corner using steps after No 109, to Mill Street. Go **R**, then **L** on to Buccleuch Road. Turn **R** following signs for riverside walk. Cross Victoria Park to join tarmac track.

❷ Turn **L** and walk by river, join road and turn **R** to cross bridge. Turn **L** along Ettrickhaugh Road, passing cottages on **L**. Just past them turn **L**, cross tiny footbridge, turn **L** down steps and follow path to river bank. Turn **R**.

❸ Follow path along river margin; it's eroded in places so watch your feet. In spring and summer your way is sprinkled with wild flowers. Eventually join wider track and bear **L**. Follow this until you reach weir and salmon ladder. Turn **R** to cross tiny bridge.

❹ Immediately after this go **L** and continue alongside river until you reach where Yarrow Water joins Ettrick Water. Retrace your steps for about 100yds (91m), then turn **L** at track crossing.

❺ Your route now goes through woods, then cross bridge by weir again. Take footpath to **L** and follow cinder/gravel track round meadow to mill buildings.

❻ Bear **R** (don't cross bridge) and continue, walking with mill lade on **L**. Where path splits, take **L** track to follow straight, concrete path beside water to abandoned fish farm.

❼ Walk around buildings, then bear **L** to continue following mill lade. Go **L** over footbridge, then **R**, passing cottages again. At main road go **R** to bridge. Don't cross bridge but join footpath on **L**.

❽ Follow this footpath past sports ground, then skirt housing estate. Continue to pedestrian footbridge on R-H side, where you cross over river, bear **R**, then retrace your footsteps back over Victoria Park and uphill to Market Place.

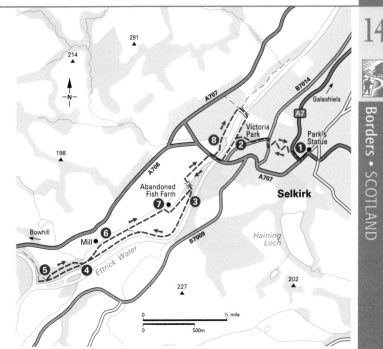

ETTRICK Going The Whole Hogg

In the footsteps of a local poet.

7 miles/11.3km 4hrs **Ascent** 420ft/1350m ⚠ **Difficulty** 2
Paths Hill tracks and grassy paths; pathless grass for Peniestone Knowe loop; 2 stiles
Map OS Explorer 330 Moffat & St Mary's Loch **Grid ref** NT 2237204
Parking On both sides of A708 near Glen Café

1 Take lane across stone bridge between 2 lochs and past Tibbie Shiels Inn, then take rougher track up through gate, with Crosscleuch Burn on **R**. It winds up to gate into plantations.

2 Fork **R** at Southern Upland Way (SUW) signpost. Path crosses footbridge, then runs up tree gap past signpost, to stile at plantation edge. It descends to footbridge over Whithope Burn, then heads up valley past ruins of Riskinhope Hope. It turns uphill, with waymarkers, to level ridgeline of Pikestone Rig. Head along ridge for 550yds (500m) to small col. Here SUW bears **L**, on to ridge flank; meanwhile another path turns sharp back **R** out of col. Later, this will be descent for Riskinhope.

3 Ignoring both paths, keep ahead up grassy ridgeline, on quad-bike track. Peniestone Knowe's plateau is rough and pathless. Summit is marked by pool, and knoll where 3 fences and fallen wall meet.

4 Don't cross any fence, but follow fence downhill to **L**. Quad-bike wheelmarks run down steep ground

with rushes, to stile where SUW crosses fence. Turn sharp **L** and follow wide, rebuilt path along flank of Peniestone Knowe to col on Pikestone Rig (Point **3**). Go slantwise through col, on to path already noted, which slants down **L** flank of ridge. On **L** is notch of Riskinhope Burn and path runs down along **R** wall. It is grassy but clear, until it passes below wide col before Peat Hill. It vanishes in boggy patch, for few steps, before reappearing on bracken slope of Peat Hill.

5 Grassy track slants down flank of Peat Hill, then zig-zags through 2 gates to valley floor meadow. Before Riskinhope House it reaches ford of Riskinhope Burn. Follow burn down to reach Loch of the Lowes.

6 Turn **R** along loch side. Go through gate above loch's corner, to bracken path. Continue alongside loch to gate at northern corner. Bear **L** to high footbridge. Cross field near river to gate on to lane beside bridge between lochs and back to start.

NEWCASTLETON Remembering The Reivers

Through borderlands where cattle raiding was once a part of everyday life.

5.75 miles/9.3km 2hrs 45min **Ascent** 689ft/210m ▲ **Difficulty** ☐
Paths Quiet byroads and farm tracks, one grassy climb
Map OS Explorer 324 Liddesdale & Kershope Forest **Grid ref** NY 483875
Parking Douglas Square

❶ From Douglas Square in centre of Newcastleton, with your back to Grapes Hotel, walk along Whitchester Street (or any other street opposite) and go down to Liddel Water. Turn **R**, then walk along river bank and join footpath downstream to reach Holm Bridge. Turn **L** at top of steps and cross bridge.

❷ After about 100yds (91m), turn **R** and follow Brampton Road, passing static. You'll eventually pass old saw mill with corrugated iron roof and will reach Tweeden Burn Bridge. Cross bridge and walk uphill, then turn **R** and join metalled track signed for Riverview Holiday Park. Continue on road until you near farm buildings.

❸ At farm entrance, fork **L** on to bed of old railway line, which has joined from **R**. This line once linked Carlisle to. Follow line as it leads past remains of Mangerton Tower, in field to **R**, and continue ahead to reach Clerkleap cottage.

❹ Walk 50yds (45m) beyond cottage and turn **L** over rotting gate. Rough path leads up **L** then turns **R**

to join rough track. This leads through woodland and uphill to join road by Sorbietrees farm. Turn **R** and walk along road, past farm, to small stand of conifers on **L**. Turn **L** through gate.

❺ Bear **R** and head up **L-H** side of trees. Walk past top of wood following dry-stone wall up below former quarry to field's top corner. Climb over field gate ahead. Now open grassy slopes lead up **L**, to cairn and fallen walls on summit of Carby Hill. Views are great from here. Known locally as Caerba Hill, this was a prehistoric settlement site.

❻ Retrace your steps to reach road again, then turn **R** and walk back past Sorbietrees farm.

❼ At farm, continue on main road as it bears **R** and follow it back over Tweeden Burn Bridge and up to Holm Bridge. Cross bridge and walk straight on for 100yds (91m), then turn **R** on B6357 and walk back to village square via heritage centre.

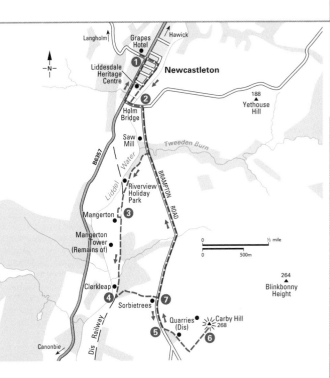

BROUGHTON John Buchan Country

A lovely walk through John Buchan country.

5 miles/8km 2hrs 30min **Ascent** 1,575ft/480m ⚠ **Difficulty** 2

Paths Hill tracks and grassy paths, 1 stile

Map OS Explorer 336 Biggar & Broughton **Grid ref** NT 119374

Parking In front of cottage past Broughton Place and art gallery

❶ From parking place, go through gate and follow obvious, grassy track running in front of cottage. Soon pass copse on **L-H** side, then pass attractively named Duck Pond Plantation, also on **L**. Track becomes slightly rougher, cross small footbridge over burn.

❷ Your track continues ahead past carpets of heather and bracken – listen for skylarks in summer. Continue walking and path soon levels out and leads past gully on **R**. Follow track until it bends, and arrive at a meeting of tracks.

❸ Take track that bears **L** and head for dip between Clover Law on **L** and Broomy Side in front. You should be able to spot fence 100yds (91m) on skyline. Make for that fence and, as you near it, you'll see a gate, next to which is wooden stile.

❹ Cross stile, then turn **R** and follow fence line. You get superb views to **L** on clear day. Continue following fence and walk up track until you reach trig point on Broughton Heights –final ascent's a bit of a puff – but it's not too long.

❺ Now retrace your steps to stile again, nip over it, but this time turn **R** and follow narrow track that climbs Clover Law. Continue walking in same direction, following fence line as it runs along ridge top. When you near end of ridge, keep your eyes peeled for path to **L**, down old earth boundary bank.

❻ Follow track as it runs down roughly in direction of cottage – it's quite steep. At bottom you'll come to old wall and burn, which you cross, then continue ahead to cross over another burn and across field to reach main track.

❼ Turn **R** here and walk past little cottage again, through gate and back to your car. To visit Broughton Place and its art gallery, continue down the track to the house on your **L**.

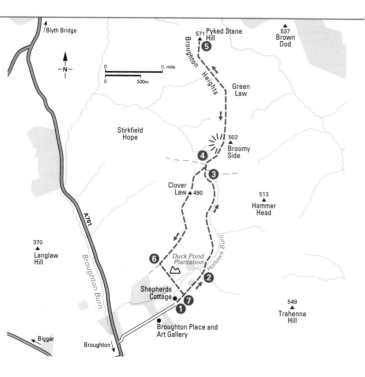

PEEBLES Birthplace Of Chambers

Discover the founders of an encyclopedia on this lovely walk.

3.5 miles/5.7km 1hr 20min **Ascent** 295ft/90m ▲ **Difficulty** ☐

Paths Waymarked riverside paths and metalled tracks

Map OS Explorer 337 Peebles & Innerleithen **Grid ref** NT 250402

Parking Kingsmeadows Road car park, Peebles

❶ Turn **R** and cross bridge. Turn **L** at Bridge Hotel and walk down slope, past swimming pool, to river. Cross small footbridge, go up some steps, turn **L**, descend steps and follow riverside track to pass a metal bridge and children's play area.

❷ Continue following obvious path and cross little bridge over burn, after which path becomes more rugged. You now enter woods, going through gate. Eventually you leave woods and come to medieval, romantic-looking Neidpath Castle on **R**.

❸ From castle continue walking by river to go through another gate. Soon on higher ground you have a view of the old railway bridge spanning the water. After another kissing gate, maintain direction to red sandstone bridge.

❹ Go up to **R** of bridge, so that you join old railway line –maintain direction and continue following Tweed Walk. Follow along this disused track until you reach Manor Bridge.

❺ Turn **L** and cross bridge, then take **L** turning signed 'Tweed Walk'. You're now on quiet lane that winds uphill –stop and look behind you for classic views of the Borders landscape. Continue until you reach track on **L** that leads into woods, opposite picnic site.

❻ Follow this path uphill, parallel to road. Just before path rejoins road, continue down wide, grassy path signposted to Peebles, with woodland to **L**. Beyond gate, path runs through fields until you join a tarmac road.

❼ Follow road and turn **L** beyond Southpark Garage into Southpark Industrial Estate, following signs to Riverside Path. Walk between units, then go down steps and bear **L** when you reach bottom. Reach footbridge ahead.

❽ Turn **R** and follow wide track beside river. This popular part of the walk attracts lots of families on sunny days. Continue walking past weir, then go up steps at bridge and cross to return to car park.

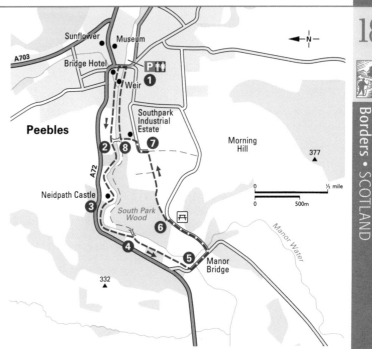

18

Borders • SCOTLAND

TRAQUAIR The Jacobite Rebellion

Jacobite connections in an atmospheric old house and a moorland fairy well.

7 miles/11.3km 3hrs 30min **Ascent**1,378ft/420m ⚠ **Difficulty** 2

Paths Firm, wide moorland tracks, 1 stile

Map OS Explorer 337 Peebles & Innerleithen **Grid ref** NT 331345

Parking Southern Upland Way car park in Traquair, near village hall

1 From Southern Upland Way car park, join tarmac road and walk **L** from Traquair village. Continue ahead and join gravel track following signs for Minch Moor. After going through gate track becomes grassier, then cross stile and enter Forestry Commission land.

2 Continue on obvious track to pass bothy on **R**. At a crossing of tracks maintain direction, crossing area of scrub and self-seeded trees. At forest track, continue ahead, taking narrow path to **R** of cycleway. Path winds uphill to rejoin cycle track at 'The Resolution Point'.

3 Maintain direction, enjoying views over Walkerburn to **L**. It feels wilder and windier here, with large tracts of heather-covered moorland. At marker post, turn **R** and walk up to cairn on Minch Moor.

4 From cairn, retrace steps back to main track. Then turn **L** and go downhill. Turn **L** 20yds (18m) beyond 'The Resolution Point' and return downhill across one forest track to reach second intersection.

5 Turn **L** now and walk downhill. Landscape soon opens out on **R-H** side giving you pleasant views of valley and river winding away. When you reach apex of bend, turn **R** along grassy path. Follow this as it bears downhill, go through gate and walk beside Camp Shiel cottage.

6 Go through another gate, cross burn, then follow grassy track and pass Damhead Shiel cottage. Go through another gate and follow path across bridge over burn. You pass expanse of scree on **R**, and ox-bow lake evolving on **L**. Cross another bridge and continue to Damhead farm.

7 Walk past farm and down to road, then turn **R**. You now cross burn again and walk past some cottages on the **R**. At war memorial on **L**, turn **R** and walk up track to the parking place at start on **L**.

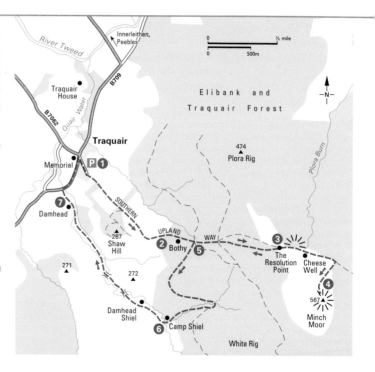

JEDBURGH Holy Orders
Pathways from a historic town.

4.5 miles/7.2km 3hrs **Ascent** 295ft/90m ⚠ **Difficulty** ①
Paths Tracks, meadow paths and some sections of road, 2 stiles **Map** OS Explorer OL16 The Cheviot Hills
Grid ref NT 651204 **Parking** Main car park by tourist information centre

❶ From car park, walk back to A68. Cross road into Duck Row. Take path on **L** to walk beside river, under old bridge, then come on to road. Turn **R** across bridge.

❷ Turn **L**, following sign for Borders Abbeys Way. Where road divides, turn **L** and follow lane beside builders' yard to join 'Waterside Walk'. When you reach main road, cross and follow tarmac lane uphill. Keep straight on, passing turning on **R**, until you reach fork, just before farmyard development on **L**.

❸ Turn **R** here to walk in front of small farmhouse called Woodend. Turn **L** on to footpath and continue past front of Mount Ulston house. Your route now runs uphill, taking you past radio mast. Maintain direction to join narrow grassy track – this can get very muddy, even in summer.

❹ Continue along track to reach fingerpost at end, then turn **L** to join St Cuthbert's Way. The going becomes much easier now on wide, firm track. At tarmac road, turn **R** and join main road. Turn **L**, go

over bridge, then cross road. Hop over crash barrier and go down steps to continue on St Cuthbert's Way.

❺ You're now on narrow, grassy track, running beside river. Cross couple of stiles, before walking across meadow frequently grazed by sheep. Walk past weir, then go through gate to cross suspension bridge – take care as it can get extremely slippery.

❻ Now pass a sign for Monteviot House and walk through woods to reach fingerpost. Turn **R** for views over river. To extend walk, continue along St Cuthbert's Way until it joins the road, then retrace your steps. Whatever you choose, retrace your steps back over suspension bridge, along riverside and back to main road. Turn **L** across bridge, then immediately **R** down a tarmac lane.

❼ Ignoring track off **L**, follow road all the way back to Jedburgh. Cross A68 and return back along 'Waterside Walk' to car park.

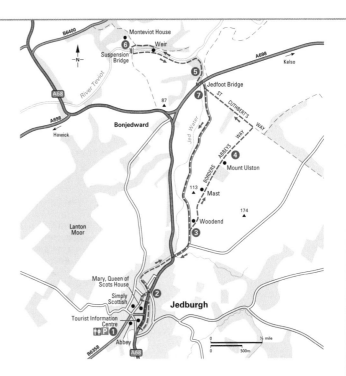

DRYBURGH A Great Scott

A gentle walk in the Borders countryside much beloved by Sir Walter Scott.

5 miles/8km 3hrs **Ascent** 131ft/40m ▲ **Difficulty** ①
Paths Firm woodland and riverside tracks, 3 stiles
Map OS Explorer 338 Galashiels, Selkirk & Melrose **Grid ref** NT 592318
Parking Dryburgh Abbey car park

❶ From abbey car park walk back to join road, pass entrance to Dryburgh Abbey Hotel and then walk down dead-end lane in front of you. You soon see river and at end of road continue along footpath and bypass, then cross bridge over River Tweed.

❷ Turn **L** immediately and join St Cuthbert's Way. This waymarked trail leads along river banks. At some points there are steps, tiny footbridges and patches of. Continue on this trail which eventually takes you past 2 small islands in river, where it then leads away from river bank.

❸ Follow trail on to tarmac track, then **L**. At main road in St Boswells go **L** again and continue to follow trail signs, passing post office and later Scott's View chippy on **L**. After house No. 101, turn **L** down Bravheads Road then go **R** along a tarmac track at end.

❹ Follow this, then turn **L** and walk past golf club house. Continue walking for a few paces, then turn **R** and follow St Cuthbert's Way as it hugs golf course. You now continue by golf course until your track

brings you back down to river bank. Walk past weir and up to bridge.

❺ Go up steps and cross bridge (take care, there is no footway), then turn sharp **L** and walk towards cottages. Before cottages, go **L**, over footbridge, then turn **R** along river bank to walk in front of them. At weir, take steps that run up to **R**, cross stile and into field.

❻ Go **L** and keep to track through woodland down to river bank, following waymarked trail.

❼ Follow the river, watching for fish leaping up to feed from water's surface. Cross stile, then pass greenhouse on **L**. Climb another stile here, turn **R**, walk past toilets and, at house ahead, turn **L** and walk back into car park.

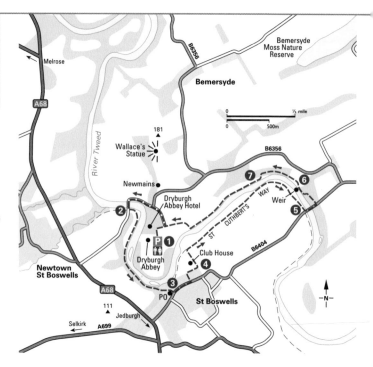

KIRK YETHOLM A Former Gypsy Village

An energetic walk over the Scottish border.

7 miles/11.3km 4hrs 30min **Ascent** 1,600ft/480m ⚠ **Difficulty** ③

Paths Wide tracks and waymarked paths, one short overgrown section, 3 stiles

Map OS Explorer OL16 The Cheviot Hills **Grid ref** NT 839276

Parking Car park outside Kirk Yetholm at junction of Pennine Way and St Cuthbert's Way

❶ Cross burn via footbridge; follow signs to St Cuthbert's Way. Bear **R** to follow track uphill, with Shielknowe Burn below on **L**. Track crosses burn, then continues uphill, skirting Green Humbleton hill and reaching fingerpost.

❷ Take grassy path on **L** to follow St Cuthbert's Way. Continue uphill; to fingerpost by wall, marking border.

❸ Follow path slantwise over ridgeline ahead, then into valley. At valley floor, cross **R-H** stream to near corner of plantation. Cross stile into forest. Path keeps near foot of trees, then joins fence by stream, before slanting slightly **R** into pine forest. Leave wood by another stile.

❹ Keep ahead across field. From far gate track starts that crosses stream, heads briefly uphill, then winds to reach Elsdonburn farm. Turn **L** between buildings and follow track round to **R**. It becomes tarred lane, with conifer wood on **L** and the burn on **R**.

❺ Follow tarred track across cattle grid to signpost. Leave St Cuthbert's Way to take tarred track on **R** signed 'Trowupburn'. Continue, passing sheepfold and conifer plantation. Track winds up, skirts hill, then descends to

Trowupburn farmhouse. Continue past farm buildings, bear **R** to fingerpost.

❻ Enter gate and follow sign 'Border Ridge 1.5'. Take this wide grassy track then cross ford next to large sheepfold. Head upstream with burn on **R**, cross burn again, cross stile and join sheep track bearing **L** through bracken.

❼ Walk round hill and, above sheepfold on **L**, bear **R** so that Wide Open burn is **L**, sheepfold behind you. Work uphill to head of burn to fence on higher ground.

❽ Enter gate at corner and take green path ahead over open ground. Walk around head of stream valley (stream drops **R**) to wall and fence marking border. Cross stile and bear **R** to Pennine Way fingerpost. Bear **L** and follow green path and waymarkers down and past fingerpost of St Cuthbert's Way (Point ❷). Keep ahead above tin shed, on path leading down to footbridge at start.

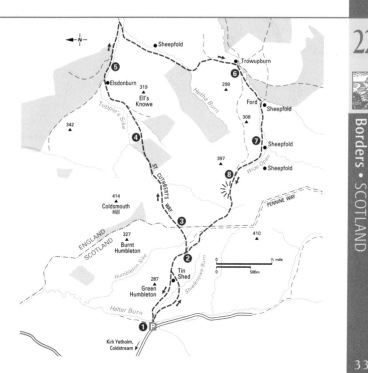

23

DUNS Stepping Back In Time

Quiet lanes through gentle countryside and past a fine Edwardian mansion.

4.5 miles/7.2km 2hrs **Ascent** 250ft/75m ⚠ **Difficulty** ☐1

Paths Mostly firm tracks and woodland paths
Map OS Explorer 346 Berwick-upon-Tweed **Grid ref** NT 787538
Parking Long-stay car park off Market Square, Duns

Borders • SCOTLAND

❶ From car park, return to Market Square and continue straight ahead up Castle Street. Cross main road to follow continuation of Castle Street, bearing **L** to enter Duns Castle Estate through an arched gateway. 50yds (46m) along drive, turn **R** up wooden steps and follow path uphill and through gate to reach summit of Duns Law.

❷ From hilltop, follow your route back down hill (sign half-way down points to alleged site of Old Duns). On reaching drive, turn **R**, then fork **R** at memorial to Duns Scotus. Follow drive along shore of Hen Poo, then fork **L** through gate on to rougher track to head of lake, where path swings **L** to reach T-junction.

❸ Turn **R** here to follow track along wooded valley and past pond, Mill Dam, which formerly provided power for estate sawmill. Shortly beyond pond, turn **L** up woodland path and continue for 100yds (91m) to footbridge crossing small stream.

❹ Turn **L** to cross bridge and climb rough timber steps. At a wooden bench, bear **R** to follow waymarked 'Colonel's Walk'. When you reach intersection, after approximately 0.5 mile (800m), turn **R** (signposted to Duns) and continue 100yds (91m) to another intersection.

❺ Turn **L** (again signed to Duns) and follow driveway until you reach crossroads. Turn **R** here, following waymarked route. After passing Duns Castle and lime avenue continue down estate road until you eventually come to main road.

❻ Turn **L** here and follow pavement back to Duns. As main road bears **L**, continue straight ahead along South Street to reach Market Square, where you turn **R** to return to car park at start of walk.

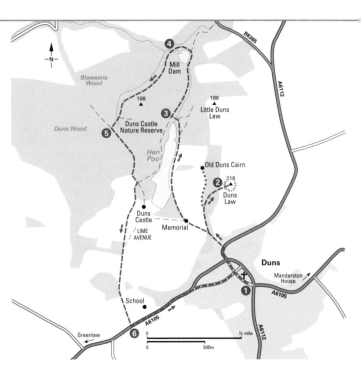

ST ABBS A Windy Walk

A refreshing walk along the cliffs where there is plenty of wildlife.

4 miles/6.4km 1hr 30min **Ascent** 443ft/135m ⚠ **Difficulty** 1

Paths Clear footpaths and established tracks
Map OS Explorer 346 Berwick-upon-Tweed **Grid ref** NT 913674
Parking At visitor centre

❶ From car park, take path that runs past information board and play area. Walk past visitor centre, then take footpath on **L**, parallel to main road. At end of path turn **L** and go through a gate –you'll immediately get great views of the sea.

❷ Follow track, pass sign to Starney Bay and continue, passing fields on your **L-H** side. Your track now winds around edge of bay – to your **R** is little harbour at St Abbs. Track then winds around cliff edge, past dramatic rock formations and eventually to some steps.

❸ Walk down steps, then follow grassy track as it bears **L**, with fence on **L**. Go up slope, through gate and maintain direction on obvious grassy track. Path soon veers away from cliff edge, past high ground on **R**, then runs up short, steep slope to crossing of tracks, passing butterfly haven on **R**.

❹ Maintain direction by keeping to coastal path which runs up slope. You'll soon get great views of St Abb's lighthouse ahead, dramatically situated on the cliff's edge. Continue to lighthouse and walk in front of lighthouse buildings and down to join tarmac road. Take care as path is steep and eroded.

❺ Follow road down to bottom of hill, then 50yds (46m) before cattle grid, turn **L** down narrow path.

❻ Continue along path and cross stile. Path now runs through scrub and woodland along edge of loch. Continue along path to intersection with track.

❼ Turn R along wide track and walk up to road. Go **L** now and continue to cross cattle grid. When you reach bend in road, follow tarmac track as it bears **L**. You'll soon go through gate, then pass some cottages before reaching car park on **L-H** side.

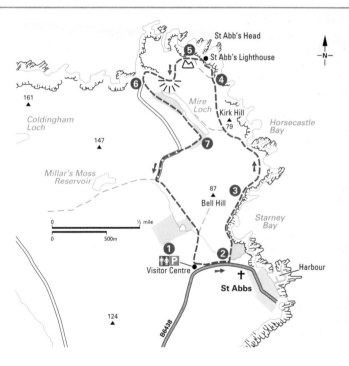

ROSLIN Romantic Roslin Glen
Tree-lined paths take you beside a river to a special ancient chapel in this glorious glen.

5 miles/8km 2hrs 30min **Ascent** 279ft/85m **⚠ Difficulty** 2
Paths Generally good, but can be muddy and slippery
Map OS Explorer 344 Pentland Hills **Grid ref** NT 272627
Parking Roslin Glen Country Park car park

❶ From country park car park, walk north-east with sound of river through trees to **L**. Go up metal stairs, cross footbridge, then walk ahead, following path uphill. In summer, you'll smell wild garlic. At bottom of steps, turn **R**, walk under old castle arch, down stone steps, then turn **L**.

❷ Follow path through scrub and up steps into dense woodland. Just by muddy burn, bear **L**, keeping to main path with gorge to **R**. Beyond line of yew trees growing from old stone wall, turn **R** and follow path that winds steeply downhill to water's edge.

❸ Walk to **L**, then follow path as it climbs again. At crossing of paths turn **R**, following direction of river. Route now takes you high above river; continue ahead to cross stile. After crossing another stile view opens out to fields on **L**, then route moves closer to river again, until you reach kissing gate.

❹ Turn **L** and follow path up steps with fields to **L**. When you reach ridge top there are good views **R**. Continue until you go through kissing gate

❺ Turn **L** and follow wide path. Eventually pass buildings of Roslin Institute, where Dolly the sheep was cloned, then pass memorial to the Battle of Rosslyn on **R-H** side. Keep walking straight ahead, through outskirts of Roslin and up to crossroads at village centre.

❻ Turn **L** here and walk ahead. Soon you see Rosslyn Chapel on the **R-H** side. If you don't intend to visit the chapel, take path that bears downhill to **R**, just in front of it. When you reach cemetery turn **L**, following signpost for Polton, and walk between cemeteries to metal gate for Rosslyn Castle. Go down steps on **R-H** side, over bridge again and return to start.

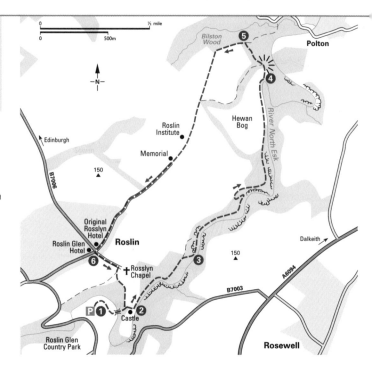

EAST LINTON Poppy Harvest

A lovely walk past an old doo'cot and a mill.

4.5 miles/7.2km 2hrs 30min **Ascent** 295ft/90m ⚠ **Difficulty** 2
Paths Field paths, river margins and woodland tracks. Short section of busy road, 3 stiles
Map OS Explorer 351 Dunbar & North Berwick **Grid ref** NT 591772 **Parking** Main street in East Linton

❶ From town-centre Market Cross take lane that to **L** of church. At main street turn **L**, then cross bridge and continue until you reach garage on **R-H** side. Turn **L** here into farm opposite garage, following sign for Houston Mill and Mill House.

❷ Follow path to **R** round farm buildings until you see the old doo'cot (dovecote). Turn **R** just in front of it and follow path along field edge. At footbridge, turn **L** to continue walking around field edge, with river on **R-H** side. At next footbridge, cross and go through metal gate.

❸ Take **R-H** path across field and go through kissing gate to reach old mill. Once you've inspected the mill continue on to meet main road, then turn **L** to walk back into town. Turn **R** to walk along High Street, then cross road and turn **L** to go down Langside.

❹ When you reach recreation ground, maintain direction and walk across grass to reach railway. Go through underpass and go ahead through fields. Continue in same direction, crossing 3 walls via steps

and 2 stiles. After you cross third wall track starts to become indistinct, but maintain direction to reach footpath sign. Bear **L** here to reach road.

❺ Turn **R** and follow paved footway through Pencraig pull-in and on to signpost to Overhailes. Turn **R** and follow it round and under dual carriageway. From farm continue down to end of lane at Hailes Mill.

❻ Don't cross bridge (unless you wish to visit the ruins of Hailes Castle) but instead follow path that runs to **L** of steps. You're now walking along river's edge on narrow path. Follow path to cross stile, walk along field margin and under new road bridge, then enter some woods. Walk up stairs, then down some steps, and continue following path to walk under another road bridge.

❼ Path now runs through garden and on to road, where you turn **R**. Walk under railway bridge, then turn **L** to return to start.

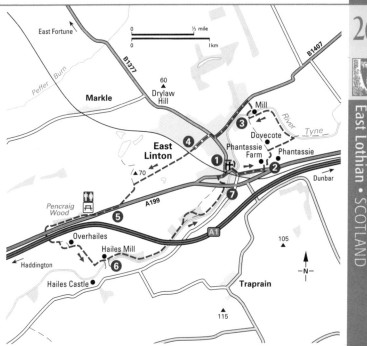

BALLANTRAE Ardstinchar Castle

The Ayrshire Tragedy, a murder most foul.

3 miles/4.8km 2hrs **Ascent** 295ft/90m ⚠ **Difficulty** ①
Paths Country lanes and farm tracks
Map OS Explorer 317 Ballantrae, Barr & Barrhill **Grid ref** NX 082824
Parking Car park near school on Foreland, Ballantrae

① Leave car park and turn **L** on to Foreland. At T-junction with Main Street cross road and turn **R**. Near outskirts, just before bridge over River Stinchar, look **L** to see ruins of former stronghold of Bargany Kennedy's Ardstinchar Castle. The castle walls are unstable so stay clear of ruins.

② Cross Stinchar Bridge and take **R** turn, heading uphill on narrow lane and past cottages. At junction keep **L** but look for a Garleffin Standing Stone in rear garden of.

③ Continue uphill passing cemetery, on **R**, then Glenapp Castle gates on **L** and then Big Park Civic Amenity Site, on **L**.

④ Next landmark on **L** is farm road to Bigpark. Continue past this and look for next farmhouse on **R**. About 300yds (274m) before house road dips; there's a stream beside road. Turn **R** on to farm track that heads downhill between high hedges.

⑤ Near hill bottom, just past large barn on **L**, road splits. Turn **R** and continue along road, through farm steading, past Downan farmhouse and uphill. When road levels look to horizon ahead for distinctive outline of Knockdolian Hill.

⑥ Look **L** at the same time to see the real Ailsa Craig to north-west. Along beach towards Ballantrae is Shellknowe. Continue along road, past farm of Kinniegar and through hamlet of Garleffin. Some houses have names like Druidslea and Glendruid.

⑦ In front garden of Druidslea is another standing stone. Turn **L**, go downhill on this country lane, turn **L** on to main road and return to Ballantrae. Go through gate on the **L-H** side and into kirkyard. Go up some steps on the **R** to find the Kennedy crypt. If door is locked look through small window on door. Return to Main Street and turn **L**, go along street and take first turning **L** past library. Walk along this street to T-junction and turn **L** into Foreland and return to start.

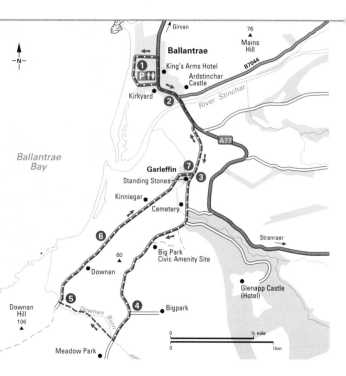

BYNE HILL Firth Of Clyde

Enjoy the views across the sea to Ailsa Craig.

3.75 miles/6km 3hrs **Ascent** 571ft/174m ⛰ **Difficulty** 2
Paths Farm roads, dirt tracks and open hillside, 1 stile
Map OS Explorer 317 Ballantrae, Barr & Barrhill **Grid ref** NX 187955
Parking Ainslie Park car park

1 From car park head south along pavement alongside A77. Pass a nursing home on **R**, then come to lane on **L** past former Shalloch mill.

2 Pavement disappears so continue along verge for 200yds (183m). Before it reappears cross bridge, turn **L** and cross road.

3 Go on to farm track alongside burn. Go over metal gate, turn **R**. Follow this newly created road running behind Woodland Farm and Ardmillan Castle Holiday Park. Pass through several metal gates. Please ensure that you always close them behind you and leave open any that are not closed.

4 Continue on to saddle between Mains Hill on **R-H** side and Byne Hill on **L**, passing remains of monument erected to memory of Archibald C B Craufurd of Ardmillan Estate. Monument is in poor repair so keep a safe distance from it. There was a plaque on the front, but some years ago this was dumped in the woods below. Turn **L** through wall gap and head up side of Byne Hill to reach prominent commemorative

cairn at summit. From this vantage point there is one of the finest views of the Firth of Clyde. On a clear day you can see the Antrim coast of Northern Ireland, the island of Arran and the Mull of Kintyre to the north and west, and, about 8 miles (12.9km) out in the sea, the distinctive outline of Ailsa Craig.

5 With cairn at your back, walk straight ahead. Cross saddle between summit and lower part of hill, keeping at first to higher ground then towards north side of hill. Descend very carefully and at bottom, turn **L** and follow wall. Continue until you pass a gate then turn **R** over stile and cross field to then go over gate on to farm road at Point **3**. From here retrace your steps to the start.

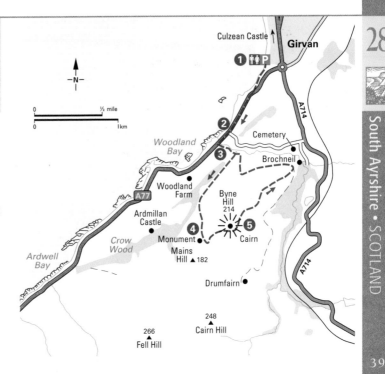

LOUDOUN Lady Flora

A tragic tale of jealousy and intrigue.

7.5 miles/12.1km 4hrs **Ascent** 187ft/57m ⚠ **Difficulty** 2
Paths Pavements, footpaths and farm roads
Map OS Explorer 334 East Kilbride Galston & Darvel **Grid ref** NS 539373
Parking On-street parking near Lady Flora's Institute

❶ Go west along Main Street; turn L into Craigview Road. Cross bridge, turn R and follow road to T-junction. Turn L; at road fork, keep R, go alongside factory, turn L into Stonygate Road and follow this to join Irvine Footpath.

❷ Keep on path, passing Strath and on to kennels. Turn R at gate and follow path round perimeter. The walkway continues along river bank on well-defined (possibly muddy) path. Continue, going through woodlands until white cottage is seen.

❸ Keep R along riverside path and cross playing fields; go through gate, then along street to T-junction.

❹ Turn R, cross road and continue, crossing 'Muckle Brig' and Galston bypass to continue on pavement heading along A719 towards Loudoun Academy. Pass academy on R, then entrance gates to Loudoun Castle.

❺ Turn L opposite gates and head along narrow lane for 0.5 mile (800m) to Loudoun Kirk Bridge. Turn L and go into Loudoun kirkyard. Return, cross small bridge and turn R on to signposted footpath to Galston. After 100yds (91m) path bends R and narrow grassy footpath forks L. Go L.

❻ Keep on this path to T-junction at Galston bypass, then turn R and head along pavement, across bridge, then turn R and head downhill. Turn L at waymarker and go through underpass to other side of bypass. Turn L and walk along footpath beside the river.

❼ At path end turn R, head along narrow lane, then turn L into Titchfield Street. Turn R at the next junction, cross road and take next L, passing 2 school buildings and cemetery to reach staggered junction. Cross B7037 and continue along Clockstone Road.

❽ Turn L at T-junction. Take next R beside house and follow road downhill, then up to pass Piersland farm. Head down and cross gate where road turns L under railway bridge. Turn R after bridge and return to start.

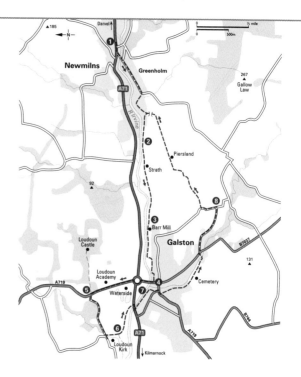

DUNASKIN The Iron Works

A hill walk to a deserted village.

4 miles/6.4km 3hrs **Ascent** 492ft/150m ⚠ **Difficulty** ③
Paths Old rail and tram beds and rough hillside
Map OS Explorer 327 Cumnock & Dalmellington **Grid ref** NX 440084
Parking Dunaskin Open Air Museum

❶ Turn **R** in front of visitor centre and follow road towards adventure playground. Go uphill on track to **R** of playground and through kissing gate into woodland. Emerge at T-junction opposite railway bridge and turn **L** on to grassy trail.

❷ When you reach metal gate across trail, go through small wooden one at its side. Climb over next gate, turn **R** and head uphill following line of disused tramway, between ends of old bridge. This is the trackbed of the former horse-drawn tramway, used to bring the iron ore down from the plateau.

❸ At hill top, when path divides, keep **L** and follow path as through 2 short sections of wall. Where path is blocked by fence, turn **R** and then go **L** to walk through gate and **R** on to metalled lane.

❹ Head along here, past remains of miners' houses of Step Row, which are clearly visible amongst trees. A stone memorial to the 'Hill stands near the site of the former village store. To the **R** of this, and now in the wood, is the former village square and remains of more houses.

❺ From stone memorial turn back towards war memorial, then return to gate at corner of wood and continue along track beside wood. In trees are the remains of Low Row. Go through another gate and continue along former railway. When it forks, keep **R**.

❻ Continue until route ahead is blocked by sheets of corrugated iron. Cross wall and turn **R**, heading downhill to pick up faint path. Continue on this to reach cluster of trees beside ruined building.

❼ Head down from here towards **R** of a row of cottages. Go through gate, turn **R** then **R** again at fork to reach Ardoon. Go past house, turn **L** on to footpath and follow it downhill and under small, disused railway bridge. Cross track and carry on, heading downhill on footpath back to visitor centre.

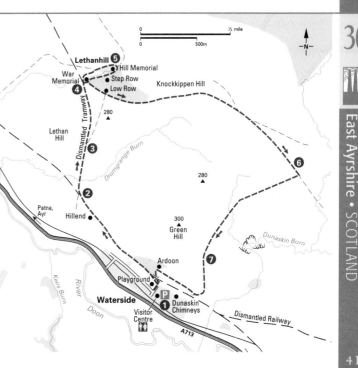

MUIRKIRK On Old Roads And Rails

Around a once-prosperous moorland town that stood at an industrial crossroads.

3.5 miles/5.7km 3hrs **Ascent** 16ft/5m **⚠ Difficulty** 1

Paths Old railway beds, farm tracks and country lanes, 1 stile
Map OS Explorer 328 Sanquhar & New Cumnock **Grid ref** NX 696265
Parking Walkers' car park, Furnace Road

1 From car park follow blue waymarker and exit car park via gate on to rough track with high wall running along to **R**. This continues as fence and, once past the end of it, look for waymarker pole on **L**.

2 Turn **L** on to grass track. Follow this to steps, go downhill and through kissing gate. Turn **R** and walk along what may have been bank of 18th-century canal.

3 Go through several kissing gates following River Ayr Way. This recently constructed path runs between 2 wire fences, along trackbed, eventually reaching kissing gate.

4 Go through gate and turn **R** on to quiet country road. Follow this past remains of old railway bridge, past farm entrance on **R** then go through gate to continue on farm road. At next gate turn **R** go through 4 gates and return to car park.

5 Turn **R** and exit car park on to Furnace Road, then turn **L**. Continue past clock tower of derelict Kames Institute and along edge of golf course. Go through gate and continue, passing cottage on **L**, on to old

drove road to Sanquhar. Go through another gate and continue to McAdam memorial.

6 Just past this head along green track on **R**. Follow this track beside stream until it joins dirt track just above Tibbie's Brig. Near here, in a small clay dwelling, lived a local poetess, Tibbie Pagan, who eked out a living by singing, selling her poetry and possibly supplying illicit whisky. She is believed locally to have been the source of 'Ca the Yowes tae the Knowes', although Burns himself collected it from a clergyman.

7 Go down to Brig and monument then return uphill keeping L on access for disabled route to McAdam's cairn. Follow this back to drove road and go L to return to car park.

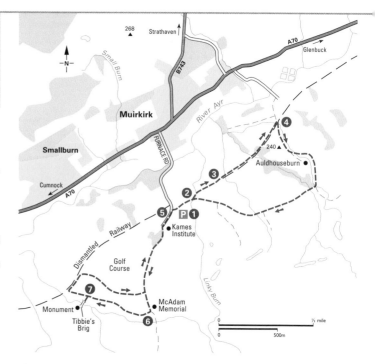

DARVEL Sir Alexander Fleming

In the footsteps of Sir Alexander Fleming.

7 miles/11.3km 3hrs **Ascent** 459ft/140m ⚠ **Difficulty** ☐2

Paths Country lanes and pavements **Map** OS Explorer 334 East Kilbride, Galston & Darvel
Grid ref NX 563374 **Parking** On-street parking at Hastings Square at start of walk

❶ From Alexander Fleming Memorial, cross square to pedestrian crossing, cross road, turn **R** and go along Main Street. Near town outskirts go across Darvel Bridge and take the second turning **L** just past John Aird factory. Go uphill on this road and pass cemetery.
❷ Keep going uphill to reach crossroads near New Quarterhouse farm. Follow waymark arrow pointing **L**. Road continues uphill, passing Henryton on **R** and then Byres on **L**. Near Byres there is bench by roadside if you want some respite on this steep climb.
❸ Little Glen is next farm on **L-H** side and shortly afterwards road forks. Take **L** turn. Next 2 farms passed on this road, in quick succession, are Meikleglen and. Just before next farm on **L**, Laigh Braidley, farm road leads off to **R**. This is entrance to Lochfield, Alexander Fleming's birthplace, which is not open to the public. Continue past Laigh Braidley.
❹ After Laigh Braidley road turns sharp **L**, then **R** and goes downhill to cross the Glen Water at Braidley Bridge. As you descend hill look slightly to **R** and

uphill and you will see steading of Lochfield, which is still farmed. Follow road uphill from bridge. There's another bench by the roadside at T-junction near hill top. Enjoy well-earned rest here and appreciate the view back across Irvine Valley.
❺ Ignore waymark and turn **L**, heading along lane and past Gateside. When road forks take **L** fork, cross Mucks Bridge and continue uphill. Lane now passes roads to Low then High Carlingcraig, then levels out. As you continue along top of hill look to **L** for distinctive outline of Loudoun Hill.
❻ When you reach Dyke road heads downhill again. Go over crossroads at Intax and continue short distance to some bungalows on **R**. Just past here take **L** turn. After Hilltop road turns sharply **R** and downhill. As you approach town lane continues into Burn Street. At T-junction turn **L** and follow this back to Hastings Square.

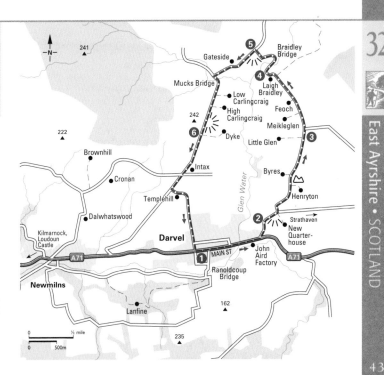

33

NEW LANARK A Revolutionary Utopia

A rustic walk from a model community.

6.5 miles/10.4km 3hrs **Ascent** 476ft/145m ⚠ **Difficulty** 2

Paths Clear riverside tracks and forest paths, a few steep steps
Map OS Explorer 335 Lanark & Tinto Hills **Grid ref** NS 883426
Parking Main car park above New Lanark

❶ From car park, walk downhill into New Lanark. Bear **L** and walk to Scottish Wildlife Trust visitor centre. Turn up stone steps on **L**, following signs to Falls of Clyde. Path soon goes down steps to reach weir and lookout point.

❷ Continue along path. You'll pass Bonnington Power Station on **R**, where it divides. Take **R-H** path, which takes you into woodland and up steps. You'll soon come to Corra Linn waterfall, with another lookout point.

❸ Your path continues to **R**, signposted 'Bonnington Linn, 0.75 miles'. Go up some more steps and follow track to go under double line of pylons. Follow path to reach weir, cross it, then turn **R** into Wildlife Reserve.

❹ After 100yds (91m), turn **R** off track down narrow path, which crosses a footbridge and then follows river, rejoining main path downstream. Bear **R** here to reach Corra Castle. Continue walking by river, cross small footbridge, then follow wide path through woods. When you meet another path, turn **R**.

❺ Follow path to pass houses on **L**. At road turn **R**, then **R** again to cross old bridge, which brings you into cul de sac. Go through gate on **R** – it looks like someone's drive but is part of Clyde Walkway.

❻ Walk past stables, then turn **L** through gate to follow riverside path. Beyond another gate, continue up steps beside water treatment plant and bear **R** along tarmac lane. Follow lane past houses until you see sign to Jooker's Johnnie on **L**. Just 20yds (18m) further on, turn **R** down driveway, then **R** again at sign for Clyde Walkway.

❼ Your path zig-zags down to river. At water's edge turn **L**, and follow forest track back to New Lanark. When path meets road turn **R**, then **L** at church for car park.

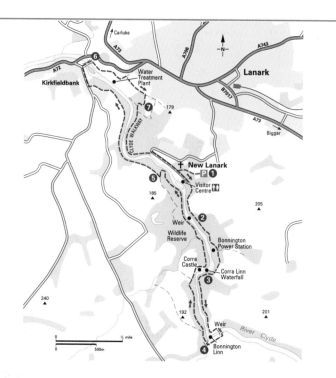

EAST KILBRIDE Kittochside Farm

An 18th-century time warp in a 20th-century new town.

5 miles/8km 3hrs **Ascent** 262ft/80m ⚠ **Difficulty** ☐

Paths Farm tracks and country roads

Map OS Explorer 342 Glasgow **Grid ref** NS 608558

Parking Car park at Museum of Scottish Country Life

❶ Exit car park and turn **R** on to road, heading past front of main Exhibition Building then turn **R** on to footpath. Continue along this, to reach T-junction.

❷ Turn **R** and follow this to another T-junction with main road. Turn **L** and continue along road, passing fields and steading of Wester Kittochside.

❸ Keep on this quiet road for just over 1 mile (1.6km), past more of fields of Wester Kittochside farm, then fields of more modern farms and finally into village of Carmunnock. Road ends at T-junction. Turn **R** then, short distance further on, take next turning on **R** into Cathkin Road.

❹ Keep on Cathkin Road for about 0.5 mile (800m) then, when it bends sharply to **L**, turn **R** and continue straight ahead on minor road. Follow this as it twists and turns to reach Highflat Farm after about 0.5 mile (800m) and then continues for another 0.5 mile (800m) to end at T-junction opposite road leading to West Rogerton farm.

❺ Turn **R** and, in just over 0.5 mile (800m), you reach crossroads. On **R** is farm track leading back to Highflat. Turn **L** here and proceed to next T-junction. Walk along this country lane passing farm of East Kittochside on **L**.

❻ Pass junction on **R**, continue through Kittochside, pass drive to Kittochside House and reach another T-junction. Cross road and continue along farm track ahead. Take first turning on **L** on to another farm track and, at end of this, you will then be back in front of museum Exhibition Building.

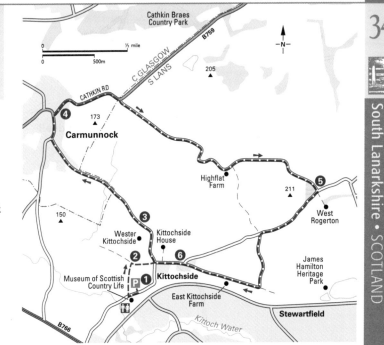

WHITING BAY The Spectacular Falls

Enjoy this short scenic woodland walk over the Isle of Arran's ancient bedrock.

2.75 miles/4.4km 2hrs **Ascent** 442ft/135m ⚠ **Difficulty** ②

Paths Forest paths and forest roads
Map OS Explorer 361 Isle of Arran **Grid ref** NS 047252
Parking Car park opposite youth hostel in Whiting Bay

❶ From car park turn **R** on to road, cross it and turn **L** on to footpath, signposted 'Giants' Graves and Glenashdale Falls'. Follow this leafy lane to rear of house, then continue on path along river bank. Go through gate, pass forest walks sign and then continue to signpost pointing in direction of Giants' Graves.
❷ Path forks here. Go **R**, following sign to Glenashdale Falls. Path continues, rising gently through wooded area, where several trees are identified by small labels on their trunks. Continue uphill on this path, which is marked by occasional waymarker, crossing bridge and fording shallow section of burn.
❸ Eventually path starts to climb steeply uphill and continues to steps and then forks. Keep **R** and follow this path to reach falls. Keep on path past falls and continue uphill to cross bridge. A picnic table on the river bank here is a good spot for refreshment.
❹ From here follow path into area planted with Sitka spruce. Keep to track marked by green waymarkers as it heads through this dark part, going through gap in

wall and eventually arrive at sign pointing to Iron Age fort. Turn off to look at rampart remains then retrace your steps to sign and continue your route along path.
❺ Cross bridge by another waterfall and then follow more waymarkers to clearing and viewpoint. From here you can see the extent of the impressive Glenashdale Falls. Waymarker points uphill through densely wooded area before ending at T-junction with forest road.
❻ Turn **R** on to forest road and continue, crossing water at ford and going through 3 kissing gates until route continues on metalled road. Continue along this road, go over crossroads and wind downhill. Turn **R** at T-junction and then walk 200yds (183m) back to start.

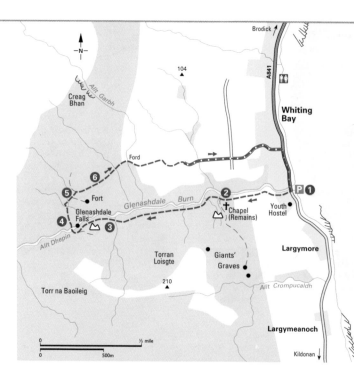

MACHRIE MOOR Arran's Standing Stones

Discover the ancient standing stones of one of Scotland's finest early settlements on the Isle of Arran.

5.5 miles/8.8km 3hrs **Ascent** 114ft/35m ⚠ **Difficulty** 1

Paths Footpaths, rough tracks, road, 3 stiles
Map OS Explorer 361 Isle of Arran **Grid ref** NS 898314
Parking King's Cave car park

❶ From car park take footpath signposted for King's Cave. This goes through area of woodland, past site of some hut circles on **R** and continues along edge of woods until it starts to head downhill towards sea. Look out for waymarker on **R** pointing back in direction you have just walked.

❷ Turn **R** here on to faint path, which in summer will be very overgrown with bracken. Plough your way through this and, in short distance, you reach wire fence, which you can easily climb through. Cross this field and go through gate, then head downhill aiming for **L** end of white cottage overlooking shore.

❸ As you near end of cottage you will see gate at corner of garden wall. Go through gate and continue along farm road running between 2 fences. Keep on this road passing another cottage on **R** and then keeping **R** at fork.

❹ When road ends at T-junction with A841 turn **L**. Continue to signpost for Machrie Moor standing stones. Turn **R**, go over stile and follow access road.

This rough track passes through 2 fields.

❺ In second field, near far **L-H** corner, is megalithic site. Nothing is to be seen above ground, the site was only identified when flints were found that were around 7,000 to 9,000 years old. Continue on road to Moss Farm road stone circle from around 2000 bc.

❻ From here track continues, passing deserted Moss Farm then crossing stile to main stone circles of Machrie Moor. When you have finished wandering around them return to stile and take Moss Farm road back to A841. Turn **L** on to this and walk for around 1.5 miles (2km) to return to car park.

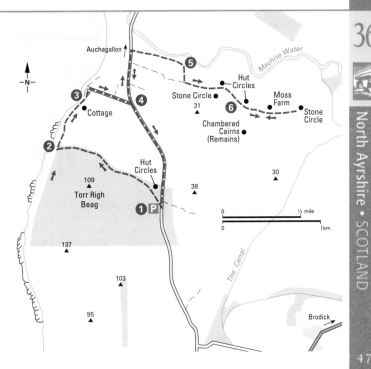

GLASGOW Alexander 'Greek' Thomson
An urban walk around a Victorian city.

6.5 miles/10.4km 3hrs 30min **Ascent** 98ft/30m ▲ **Difficulty** 2
Paths Pavements **Map** OS Explorer 342 Glasgow; AA Street by Street **Grid ref** NS 587653
Parking Sauchiehall Street multi-storey or on-street parking

❶ Exit Central Station; turn **R**. At junction with Union Street turn **R**. Building on opposite corner is the Ca' d'Oro building based on the Golden House in Venice. The upper storeys are made of cast iron. A little way down Union Street from here on the same side as the Ca' d'Oro is Thomson's Egyptian Halls.

❷ Cross then head down Union Street turning **L** into Argyle Street at next junction. Cross Argyle Street, then walk along to junction with Dunlop Street to Buck's Head. Cross Argyle Street again, retrace your steps, turning **R** into Buchanan Street. Turn **L** into Mitchell Lane, pass Lighthouse, turn **R**.

❸ Walk up Mitchell Street, continue along West Nile Street then turn **L** into St Vincent Street. Continue for just under 0.5 mile (800m), going uphill to junction with Pitt Street. You are now in front of 'Greek' Thomson's St Vincent Street church. Cross St Vincent Street then head up Pitt Street to Sauchiehall Street.

❹ On opposite corner is Thomson's Grecian Chamber (1865) and to **R** along Scott Street is Rennie

Mackintosh's Glasgow School of Art. From front of Grecian Chamber turn **L**, head down Sauchiehall Street to Charing Cross; take pedestrian bridge over motorway to Woodlands Road. Go along until it ends at Park Road, turn **R**, then **L** into Great Western Road.

❺ Go **R** on Belmont Street, **L** at Doune Gardens, continue along Doune Quadrant, then **L** again at Queen Margaret Drive. Cross road and head down past Botanic Gardens to turn **R**, back into Great Western Road. Cross road and continue to Thomson's Great Western Terrace. Trace your steps back from here to top of Byres Road and turn **R**, near bottom, turn **L** into University Avenue.

❻ Go **L** into Oakfield Avenue, pass Eton Terrace on corner with Great George Street. Turn **R** into Great George Street, **R** at Otago Street, **L** into Gibson Street and keep going when it becomes Eldon Street. Turn **R** into Woodlands Road and return to Sauchiehall Street. Follow this to junction with Renfield Street, turn **R** and head downhill to Central Station.

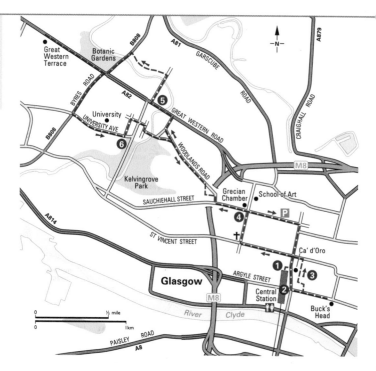

CLYDESIDE Harbour's Tall Ship
The last of the Clyde-built sailing ships.

4.75 miles/7.7km 3hrs 30min **Ascent** 98ft/30m ⚠ **Difficulty** 1
Paths Pavements and footpaths
Map OS Explorer 342 Glasgow; AA Street by Street **Grid ref** NS 569652
Parking SECC car park beside Clyde Auditorium (Armadillo)

❶ From Scottish Exhibition and Conference Centre (SECC) car park go on to Clyde Walkway and turn **R**, following signs to The Tall Ship' and Museum of Transport (leave route along here to visit the Glenlee). At the roundabout with Tall Ship on the **L**, go over pedestrian bridge to cross Clydeside Expressway. Go under a bridge into Kelvin Haugh Street.

❷ Turn west into York Hill Street, then **R** into Haugh Road and keep ahead, crossing Sauchiehall Street and then along Kelvin Way.

❸ Pass recently restored Kelvingrove Art Gallery and Museum on **L**. This is Scotland's top tourist attraction and is free.

❹ Turn **R** on to Kelvin Walkway, **R** again over second bridge, then **L** at the Memorial to Highland Light Infantry. Fork **L** and follow river bank.

❺ This eventually goes uphill. Just before top of hill look for narrow path on **L**. Go **L** here and under bridge. Turn **L** at cycle path sign to Woodside and Milngavie, go over bridge and past café/bar then

continue along walkway.

❻ Cross another bridge, go **L** at junction, still following river. Go under bridge and then **L** across humpback bridge leading to Botanic Gardens. Head up steps to reach gardens. Turn **R** alongside Kibble Palace, turn **L** and follow this drive to gates and then exit gardens.

❼ Cross Great Western Road at traffic-lights and walk to end of Byres Road. Cross Dumbarton Road and turn **L** into Partickridge Street, **R** into Dunaskin Street, **L** at T-junction then **R** into Ferry Road. Just before railway bridge turn **L** on to footpath. At its junction with Sandyford Street turn **R** and continue under bridge and back to SECC.

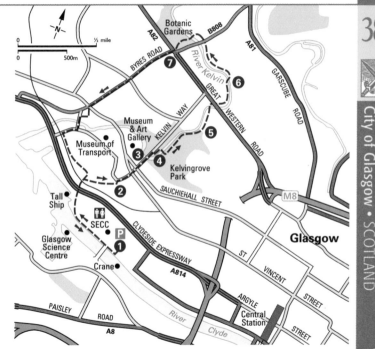

KILSYTH Along The Wall

Travel back in time by walking along an 18th-century canal and then a section of the Antonine Wall.

3.5 miles/5.7km 3hrs **Ascent** 344ft/105m ▲ **Difficulty** 1
Paths Tow path, farm road, footpath and road
Map OS Explorer 348 Campsie Fells **Grid ref** NS 719770
Parking Car park near old quarry at Kilsyth

❶ Leave car park on to main road and turn **R**. Cross road and turn immediately **L** on to road signposted for Twechar and Kirkintilloch. Continue along this road for short while and, when it turns sharply **R**, veer off footpath to **L** and on to tow path of Forth and Clyde Canal.

❷ Go round barrier and keep on along tow path until it rejoins pavement beside main road. Take next turning on **L**, cross canal via bridge and enter Twechar. Continue on this road, heading uphill; near top look for sign on **L** pointing to Antonine Wall and Bar Hill.

❸ Take next turning on **L** on to access road. Continue along here past houses and continue on farm track. Go through gate and uphill. Look back the way you have come for a grand view of the canal as it winds its way towards Glasgow.

❹ When you reach entrance to Antonine Wall go **L** through kissing gate and along grassy lane, then go through another kissing gate to access site. Veer **L** and uphill to Bar Hill Fort. From the top of the fort you will

see some woodland in front of you. Head for opening in trees and then on to well-defined trail.

❺ Follow this trail through trees, then up on to summit of Castle Hill. From here head downhill with remains of Roman Antonine Wall on your **L-H** side. Turn **R** when your path is blocked by dry-stone wall and follow it until you intersect farm track.

❻ Turn **L** and follow this through 2 kissing gates to reach T-junction with main road. Turn **L** and head down hill. Keep **R** at roundabout, still heading downhill to reach another T-junction. From here cross over road and re-enter car park.

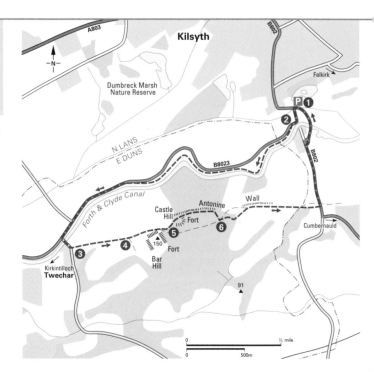

PENTLAND HILLS Soldiers And Saints

Across the hills near Edinburgh's reservoirs.

7 miles/11.3km 3hrs **Ascent** 837ft/255m ⚠ **Difficulty** 2

Paths Wide firm tracks, short stretches can be muddy, 3 stiles
Map OS Explorer 344 Pentland Hills **Grid ref** NT 212679
Parking Car park at end of Bonaly Road, beyond Bonaly Tower

❶ From car park, go through gate and take **R-H** path, signposted Tordruff Reservoir. Beyond wooden gate, path crosses over reservoir dam to intersect with tarmac lane.

❷ Turn L along lane, keeping Torduff Reservoir on **L**. At top of reservoir, cross little bridge and follow metalled track as it bends round to **R** beside waterfall. Walk under line of electricity pylons, and cross small bridge, passing water chute on **L-H** side, and continue past Clubbiedean Reservoir.

❸ Your path now bears **R**, between fields. Pass under another line of pylons and walk to Easter Kinleith farm. Now follow lane as it bends back to **L**, signposted 'Harlaw'. Pass sign for Poets' Glen and continue ahead, over bridge and on to large white house (Crossroads) on **L-H** side.

❹ Turn **L**. Follow track past conifer plantation on **L-H** side, then go through small gate. Continue walking ahead until to intersection. Turn **L** through gate, signposted to Glencorse.

❺ Follow path across moor and into hills, where you cross stone stile. Continue in same direction until you reach copse of conifers on **R-H** side, with Glencorse Reservoir ahead. Turn **L**, following sign to Colinton by Bonaly.

❻ Walk uphill and maintain direction to go through metal gate. Track now narrows and runs through hills, until it eventually opens out. Continue in same direction to reach fence encircling conifers. Keep fence on **L** and walk down to gate on **L-H** side.

❼ Turn **L** through gate. Walk past Bonaly Reservoir, then through kissing gate and walk downhill, getting good views over Edinburgh as you descend. When you reach wooden gate, go through and continue ahead, downhill, with trees on either side. Go through another kissing gate and follow tarmac path ahead to return to car park.

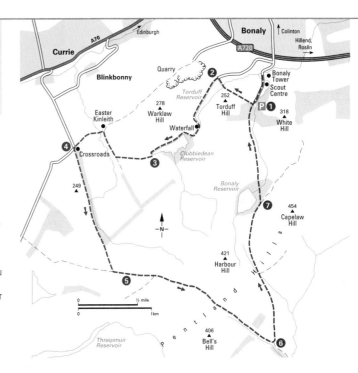

EDINBURGH OLD TOWN Murky Secrets

Through Edinburgh's Old Town.

2 miles/3.2km 1hr **Ascent** 197ft (60m) ⚠ **Difficulty** ①
Paths City streets, some hill tracks **Map** AA Street by Street Edinburgh **Grid ref** NT 256739
Parking Several NCP car parks in Edinburgh

❶ From main entrance to Waverley Station, turn **L**, go to end of street, then cross over and walk up Cockburn Street to Royal Mile, where you turn **L** and walk downhill. Continue to black gates of Holyroodhouse. Turn **R** and walk to face new Parliament visitor centre.
❷ Turn **L** and follow road to **R**, then turn **R** again past Dynamic Earth (the building looks like a huge white woodlouse) and walk up into Holyrood Road. Turn **L**, walk past new buildings of newspaper, The Scotsman, and walk up to St Mary's Street, where you turn **R** and rejoin Royal Mile. Were you to continue ahead you would join Cowgate, some parts of which were devastated by fire in December 2002.
❸ Turn **L**, to main road, then turn **L** along South Bridge. At Chambers Street turn **R** and walk past museums. At end of road, cross and then turn **L** to see the little statue of Greyfriars Bobby, the dog that refused to leave this spot after his master died.
❹ You can now cross road and make short detour into Greyfriars Kirk to see where Greyfriars Bobby

is buried close to his master. Or simply turn **R** and walk down Candlemaker Row. At bottom, turn **L** and wander into atmospheric Grassmarket – filled with shops and lively restaurants.
❺ When you've explored Grassmarket, walk up winding Victoria Street (it says West Bow at the bottom). About two-thirds of the way up look for steps hidden away on **L**. Climb them and walk ahead at top to join Royal Mile again.
❻ Turn **L** to walk up and visit castle. Then walk down Royal Mile again, taking peek into the dark wynds (alleyways) that lead off it. You eventually pass St Giles' Cathedral on **R**, which is well worth a visit.
❼ Next on your **L** you pass City Chambers (under which lies mysterious Mary King's Close). Continue until you reach junction with Cockburn Street. Turn **L** and walk back down this winding street. At bottom, cross road and return to entrance to Waverley Station.

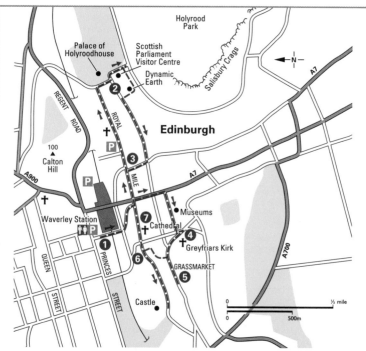

EDINBURGH NEW TOWN Luring The Literati

A walk in the footsteps of literary giants.

3 miles/4.8km 1hr 30min **Ascent** 164ft/50m ⚠ **Difficulty** ☐2

Paths Busy city streets **Map** AA Street by Street Edinburgh **Grid ref** NT 257739

Parking Several large car parks in central Edinburgh

❶ From tourist information centre, turn **L** and walk along Princes Street. Pass Scott Monument on **L**, cross road to reach Jenners department store. Continue along Princes Street; take **R** turn up Hanover Street.
❷ Take second turning on **L** and walk along George Street to reach elegant Charlotte Square. Turn **R** and **R** again to go along Young Street. At end, turn **L** and walk down North Castle Street to reach Queen Street.
❸ Cross road, turn **L**, then **R** down Wemyss Place and **R** into Heriot Row. When you reach Howe Street turn **L** and, before you reach church in middle of street, turn **L** and walk along South East Circus Place. Walk past sweep of Royal Circus and then down into Stockbridge.
❹ Cross bridge, then turn **L** along Dean Terrace. At end, turn **R** into Ann Street. When you reach Dean Park Crescent turn **R** and follow road round into Leslie Place and into Stockbridge again. Cross main road, turn **L** and then **R** at traffic lights down St Bernard's Row. Follow this, then bear **L** into Arboretum Avenue.

❺ Follow this road past Water of Leith down to Inverleith Terrace. Cross and walk up Arboretum Place to Botanic Gardens entrance on **R**. Turn **L** after visiting gardens and retrace your steps to Stockbridge.
❻ Turn **L** at Hectors bar and walk uphill; turn **L** along St Stephen Street. At church follow road, cross over Cumberland Street then turn **L** along Great King Street. At end, turn **R**, then immediately **L** to walk along Drummond Place, past Dublin Street and continue ahead into London Street.
❼ At roundabout turn **R** and walk up Broughton Street to reach Picardy Place. Turn **L**, walk past statue of Sherlock Holmes, then bear **L** towards Playhouse Theatre. Cross, continue **L**, then turn **R** into Leopold Place and **R** again into Blenheim Place. At church turn **R**, walk up steps and turn **L** at meeting of paths.
❽ Go up steps on **R**, walk over Calton Hill, then turn **R** to pass canon. Go downhill, take steps on **L** and walk into Regent Road. Turn **R** and walk back into Princes Street and start.

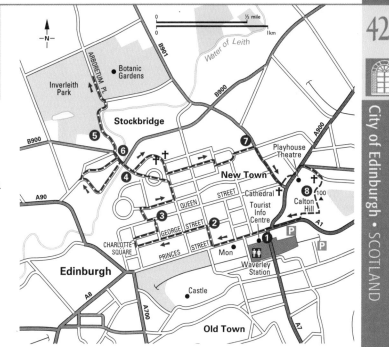

LEITH Intoxicating Memories
Along the river to Edinburgh's ancient port.

3.5 miles/5.7km 1hr 30min **Ascent** Negligible ▲ **Difficulty** 1
Paths Wide riverside paths and city streets
Map OS Explorer 350 Edinburgh **Grid ref Start** NT 243739 **Finish** NT 271766
Parking Scottish National Gallery of Modern Art, Belford Road

❶ From junction of Dean Bridge and Queensferry Street, turn **L** down Bell's Brae. You are now in the Dean Village, which dates back to 1128. At bottom, turn **R** into Miller Row.

❷ Follow this under Dean Bridge, designed by Thomas Telford. Your path then runs along bottom of steep-sided gorge, beside Water of Leith, and feels extremely rural. You'll pass an old well on your **L**, followed by the more impressive St Bernard's Well.

❸ St Bernard's Well was discovered by schoolboys in 1760. The water was said to have healing properties and, in 1789, the Roman Temple was built. From here continue along main path, then climb steps. Turn **L**, and go **R** on to Dean Terrace to reach Stockbridge.

❹ Cross road and descend steps – immediately **R** of building with clock tower. Continue to follow path beside river. Where path ends, climb on to road, turn **L** and then **R** to go down Arboretum Avenue.

❺ Walk along road, then turn **R** along path marked 'Rocheid Path'. This runs beside the river and is a popular cycleway and jogging path. Follow this, passing backs of Colonies. This low-cost housing was built by the Edinburgh Co-operative for artisans living here in the late 19th century. The idea was to provide houses in a healthy environment.

❻ Go **R**, over bridge, climb steps, then turn **L**, walking towards clock tower. At end turn **L** along Warriston Place, cross road, then turn **R** down Warriston Crescent. This is lined with town houses. Walk to end where you reach playing fields.

❼ Bear **R**, around edge of park, then follow path as it bears uphill between trees. Turn **L** at top and follow cycle track marked 'Leith 1.25'. Follow this all the way into Leith, where it brings you out near old Custom House. Cross bridge, then turn **L** to walk along the shore and explore, before returning to town by bus.

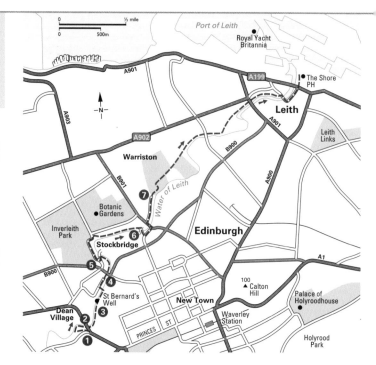

FALKIRK Reinventing The Wheel

Along the canal to a 21st-century waterwheel

2 miles/3.2km; 4 miles/6.4km with monument 1hr **Ascent** 197ft/60m ⚠ **Difficulty** 1

Paths Canal tow paths and town streets
Map OS Explorer 349 Falkirk, Cumbernauld & Livingston **Grid ref** NS 868800
Parking Car park at Lock 16, by Union Inn

❶ Start at Union Inn by Lock 16. This was once one of the best-known pubs in Scotland. Turn **R** now, away from canal, then go **R** along road. Turn **R** along Tamfourhill Road and go through kissing gate on **L-H** side of road. Alternatively, don't turn up Tamfourhill Road, but continue walking uphill to go under viaduct. Keep walking to monument on **L**. This commemorates the Battle of Falkirk (1298) in which William Wallace was beaten by Edward I's troops. Retrace your steps, under viaduct, turn **L** into Tamfourhill Road, and **L** through kissing gate on **L-H** side.

❷ This takes you to section of Antonine Wall with deep ditch and rampart behind it. Walk parallel with Tamfourhill Road. At end climb up bank on **R-H** side and down steps to join road by kissing gate.

❸ Go **L** to continue along road to another kissing gate **L** leading you to much shorter section of wall. Leave wall, rejoin road and maintain direction to mini-roundabout. Turn **L**, along Maryfield Place. At end, join public footpath signed to canal tow path and

woodland walks. Follow this track as it winds up and over railway bridge, then on to reach Union Canal.

❹ Don't cross canal but turn **R** and walk along tow path. Eventually reach Roughcastle tunnel – it currently closes at 6pm.

❺ Walk through tunnel – it's bright and clean and dry – to new Falkirk Wheel (and another section of Antonine Wall). You can walk to Wheel, then walk down to visitor centre at bottom. Bear **R** from here to cross bridge over Forth and Clyde Canal.

❻ Turn **R** now and walk along tow path. Lots of dog walkers and cyclists come along here (so take care if you are walking with a dog), while people frequently go canoeing along the canal. Keep walking until you come back to Lock 16, then turn **R** and cross canal again to return to the start at Union Inn.

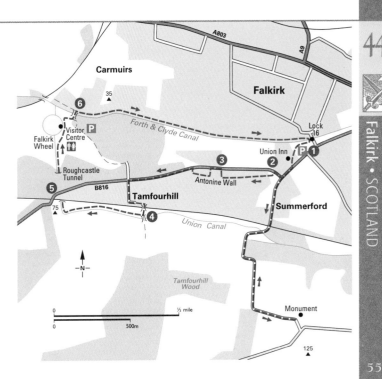

BENMORE A Botanic Garden

Discover the story of James Duncan, the man who altered the Cowal landscape.

4 miles/6.4km 2hrs 30min **Ascent** 459ft/140m 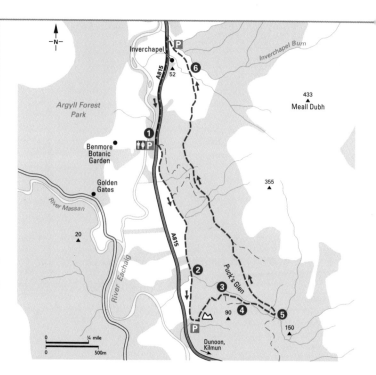 **Difficulty** 1

Paths Mainly forest roads and well-made footpaths, 1 stile
Map OS Explorer 363 Cowal East **Grid ref** NS 142855
Parking Car park at Benmore Botanic Garden

❶ From car park cross A815 and follow footpath past waymarker for Black Gates. Pass sign for Big Tree Walk and turn **R** on to surfaced lane. Continue along this lane for about 1 mile (1.6km) and just after parapet of bridge is first footpath, which leads to Puck's Glen on **L**.

❷ Milestone here points to 'Dunoon Pier 6 miles'. Ignore this entrance and continue along lane until you reach car park. Turn **L** and along footpath past waymarker pole for Puck's Glen. Climb uphill on steep path.

❸ At top of hill path levels out then starts to head back downhill, rather steeply on series of steps with handrails to bottom of gorge. Signpost found at junction at bottom of steps points **L** for lower gorge and **R** for upper.

❹ Turn **R**, head downhill on another set of steps, then cross bridge on **L** and turn **R** to head along footpath on opposite side of stream. Head uphill, cross another bridge, then go past series of small waterfalls.

Eventually reach another bridge to cross before coming to steps that take you up steep part of hillside to another bridge at top. After crossing it path levels out slightly and continues through trees to then reach T-junction with forestry road.

❺ At junction is waymarker post. Turning **R** will lead you along forest road to Kilmun Arboretum. However, for this walk you must turn **L**, following signs for Black Gates. Forestry Commission has installed new footpaths and this route can be shortened by taking any downhill paths on **L**.

❻ Follow signs to **L** and go on to path for Black Gates car park and, from there, return to botanic gardens. Otherwise continue on forest road until you reach gate near its end. Continue to reach T-junction and then turn **L** on to A815. Walk along for 0.5 mile (800m) to return to the start.

DUNARDRY FOREST Around Mòine Mhòr

A canal and Scotland's last wild peat bog.

8.25 miles/13.3km 5hrs **Ascent** 176ft (55m) ⚠ **Difficulty** ☒

Paths Canal tow path, country roads and farm tracks
Map OS Explorer 358 Lochgilphead & Knapdale North **Grid ref** NR 824908
Parking Dunardry Forest car park

❶ From car park go down steps, cross road and turn **L**. Continue to white cottage on **R**. Turn **R** on to dirt track behind cottage; go through gap between fence and wall. Cross canal over Dunardry Lock and turn **L** on to tow path.

❷ Follow tow path to Bellanoch Bridge; turn **R** on to road, cross Islandadd Bridge and on to B8025. This long, straight narrow road runs **R** through Mòine Mhor. Continue for nearly 2 miles (3.2km) then turn **R** on to unclassified road signposted for Drimvore.

❸ Continue for about 1.75 miles (2.8km) through National Nature Reserve and pass farms of Dalvore and Drimvore. Finally reach T-junction with A816 and turn **R**. After 0.5 mile (800m) Historic Scotland fingerpost points in direction of Dunadd Fort.

❹ Turn **R** here on to long straight farm road and continue, passing farm of Dunadd, to Historic Scotland car park. Make your way towards hill on well-trodden path, pass house on **L** and through kissing gate. Continue on path, following direction arrows, to

emerge through gap in rocks within outer ramparts.

❺ Continue to summit and then return by same route to car park. Leave it and turn **R** on to farm track. Go through gate then, almost immediately, go **L** through another gate and follow it as it curves **L**.

❻ Another gate is encountered just before road turns **R** and heads uphill. Follow road going through another gate to steading of Dunamuck farm. Turn **L** through steading, go through gate and head downhill on farm road, continuing until you reach T-junction with A816.

❼ Turn **R** on to road and follow it for about 0.5 mile (800m), then turn **R** on to road signposted for Cairnbaan and Crinan. After 0.25 mile (400m) turn **R** towards Crinan. As road turns **L** across swing bridge keep ahead and on to tow path. Follow this back to Dunardry Lock and retrace your steps to car park.

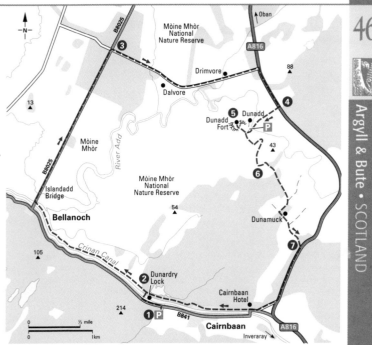

KILMARTIN GLEN Neolithic Monuments

A short walk to the stone shrines and monuments in the valley of the ghosts.

3.5 miles/5.7km 3hrs **Ascent** Negligible ⚠ **Difficulty** ☐1
Paths Boggy fields, old coach road and country lanes, 3 stiles
Map OS Explorer 358 Lochgilphead & Knapdale North **Grid ref** NR 835988
Parking Car park outside Kilmartin church

❶ From car park visit Kilmartin church to see stones and Kilmartin Cross. Leave church, turn **L** and walk along road past Kilmartin House, exit village and head downhill towards garage on **L**. Just before garage turn **L**, go through kissing gate and head across field to Glebe Cairn.

❷ From cairn head half **R**, across field to cross stile. In wet weather this can be very boggy so stout footwear is advisable. Cross stream by bridge. Go through gate and turn **L** on to old coach road. Follow this to next cairn. Go **L** over stile and follow path to visit cairn.

❸ Return to road and turn **L**, continuing to next cairn. After exploring, follow coach road to Kilmartin school, where route becomes metalled road. Go through crossroads, past Nether Largie farm and, ignoring cairn on **L**, continue short distance to Temple Wood ahead on **R**.

❹ Go through gate on **R** into Temple Wood, then return by same route. Turn **R** on to road and continue

until you reach T-junction. Turn **L** and walk along road to sign on **R** for Ri Cruin Cairn. Cross wall via stile and proceed along well-defined path to ancient monument.

❺ Return by same route and turn **R** on to road. Follow it to T-junction then turn **L** and keep ahead to car park at Lady Glassary Wood. Opposite this take path to **L** signposted to Temple Wood. Cross bridge, go through gate and head towards standing stones.

❻ Turn **R** and walk across field away from stones towards wood. Go through gate and follow fenced path to Nether Largie Cairn. From here continue along fenced path, go through another gate and turn **R** on to road. Continue past Nether Largie farm and Kilmartin school and retrace your steps to reach Kilmartin church and car park.

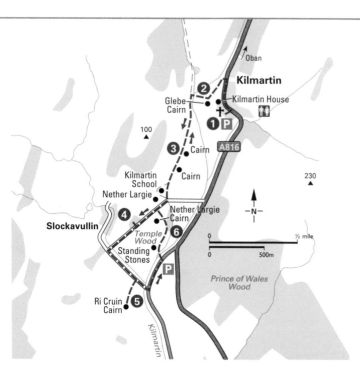

CRUACHAN The Hill With The Hole

Along Loch Awe from Cruachan Reservoir.

2 miles/3.2km 1hr 45min **Ascent** 1,200ft/365m ⚠ **Difficulty** ③
Paths Steep rugged paths, 2 ladder stiles **Map** OS Explorer 377 Loch Etive & Glen Orchy
Grid ref NN 078268 **Parking** Two pull-ins on north side of A85, below railway station. Also lay-by
0.5 mile (800m) west. Not visitor centre car park

❶ Two paths run up on either side of Falls of Cruachan. Both are initially rough and steep through woodland. The western one starts at tarred lane opposite entrance to power station proper (not visitor centre, slightly further to west). This diminishes to track, which becomes rough and crosses railway as level crossing. Path continues uphill in steep zig-zags through birch, rowan and oak. There are various points to stop and admire Loch Awe, which disappears into distance. White speckled stones in path are Cruachan granite. Path continues on steeply to top of wood.
❷ Here high ladder stile crosses deer fence. With stream on your **R**, continue uphill on small path to track below Cruachan dam. Turn **L**, up to base of dam, which measures 1,030ft (315m) wide and 150ft (46m) high. Because it's tucked back into corrie, it can't be seen from below, but it is clearly visible from top of Dun na Cuaiche, 12 miles (19.3km) away. The hollows between the 13 huge buttresses send back fine echo. Steps on **L** lead up below base of dam, then iron steps

take you on to dam's top.
❸ From here you can look across reservoir and up to skyline that's slightly jagged at back **L** corner, where Ben Cruachan's ridge sharpens to rocky edge. In other direction, your tough ascent is rewarded by long view across Lorn. Turn **R** to dam end, where track leads down **R** to junction, then **R** for 50yds (46m).
❹ At this point you could stay on track to cross concrete bridge just ahead, leading to top of path used for coming up. Otherwise there is clear path as you go down to **L** of stream, to reach a high, steep ladder stile. (Dog flap in deer fence alongside.) Below this there is clear path that descends grassy slopes and gives good view of some of Falls of Cruachan. Inside wood, path becomes steep and rough for rest of the descent. Just above railway, it turns **L**, then passes under line by low tunnel beside Falls of Cruachan Station, to A85.

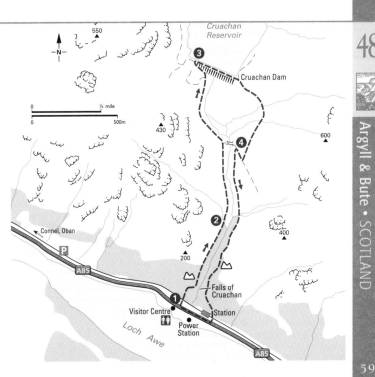

IONA Holy Island Of St Columba

A circuit of Iona to the marble quarry and Coracle Bay.

5.25 miles/8.4km 3hrs 30min **Ascent** 650ft/198m ⚠ **Difficulty** ③
Paths Tracks, sandy paths, some rugged rock and heather
Map OS Explorer 373 Iona, Staffa & Ross of Mull **Grid ref** NM 286240
Parking Ferry terminal at Fionnphort on Mull

❶ Ferries cross to Iona about every hour. On island, take tarred road on **L**, passing Martyr's Bay. After second larger bay, rejoin road as it bends **R**. Follow road across island to gate on to Iona golf course (dogs on leads).

❷ Take sandy track ahead; bear **L** past cairn to shore. Turn **L** along shore to large beach. At its end, bear **L** up narrow valley. After 100yds (91m) pass small concrete hut to join stony track. It passes fenced reservoir and drops to corner of Loch Staoineig. Walk along to the **L** of lochan on path, improved in places, that runs gently down to Coracle Bay. Cross to **L** of furrows of lazybeds cultivation – fields drained to improve crop yields –and reach shore just **L** of rocky knoll.

❸ Take route ahead following indistinct path. If your ferry to mainland leaves in 2 hours time or earlier, return by outward route and explore marble quarries on another visit. Otherwise, return inland for 200yds (183m) and bear **R** into little grassy valley. After 100yds (91m), go through broken wall and then bear slightly

L, past another inlet on **R**. Cross heather to island's eastern shoreline. Bear **L**, above small sea cliff, for 0.25 mile (400m). Turn sharp **R** into little valley descending into remnants of marble quarry.

❹ Turn inland, back to valley head. Pass low walls of 2 ruined cottages and for about 200yds (183m) to fence corner. Keep fence on **L**, picking through heather, rock and bog. Dun I with its cairn appears ahead – aim for it to reach edge of fields, where fence runs across ahead. Turn **R** along it to a small iron gate.

❺ This leads to track that passes Ruanaich farm to tarred road of outward walk. Cross on to farm track, which bends to **R** at Maol. It reaches Baile Mor (Iona village) at ruined nunnery. Just ahead is abbey with its squat square tower, or turn **R** directly to return to ferry pier.

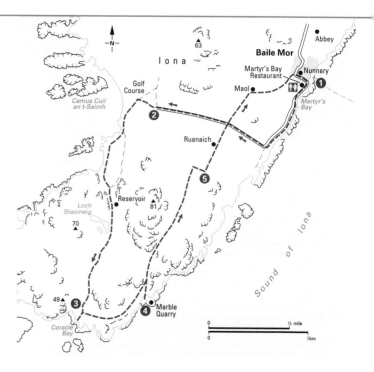

INVERARAY The Castle Of Cups

Enjoy a fine view of Inveraray.

4miles/6.4km 2hrs 15min **Ascent** 900ft/274m ⚠ **Difficulty** ②

Paths Clear, mostly waymarked paths, no stiles

Map OS Explorer 363 Cowal East **Grid ref** NN 096085 **Parking** Pay-and-display, Inveraray Pier

❶ Follow seafront past Argyll Hotel and bear **L** towards Inveraray Castle. At first junction, turn **R** past football pitch with standing stone. After coach park on **L** and end wall of castle on **R**, estate road on **L** is signed 'Dun na Cuaiche Woodland Walks'. It passes a memorial to clansmen who were killed for religious reasons in 1685. Cross stone-arched Garden Bridge to junction.

❷ Half-**R** now is the uphill path with coloured waymarkers that will be return leg of walk. During summers this may be affected by timber lorries, when there will be notice closing this path. If you see notice, it is fine to continue with route described below up to Dun na Cuaiche, Point ❹, before returning by way up, via Point ❸. Turn **R** on riverside track and follow it to picnic table with view back to castle. Rough track runs up **L**, but turn off on to small path just **R** of this, beside stone gatepost. It climbs steeply through area where attempts have failed to eradicate rhododendron.

❸ At green track above, turn **R**, slightly uphill to turning circle. Turn **L** up a muddy path under trees. This improves, bending **L** and slanting uphill across stream. Path continues uphill under trees, with stream nearby on its **L** through woods. As slope eases, path crosses clearing to meet wider one. Turn **L**, in zig-zags, to summit of Dun na Cuaiche.

❹ Return down path to clearing, but this time keep ahead. Path, rather muddy, bends **L** then enters plantation and becomes clear track. It passes between 2 dry-stone pillars where wall crosses, turns back sharp **L**, and passes between 2 more pillars lower down same wall. Continue down track, ignoring side-tracks on **L**, to lime kiln on **R**.

❺ Past lime kiln, gate leads into field. Fork **R** off track, re-crossing it below to gate beyond. This leads into wood. Path runs down to track junction before Garden Bridge (Point ❷). Return along castle driveway to Inveraray.

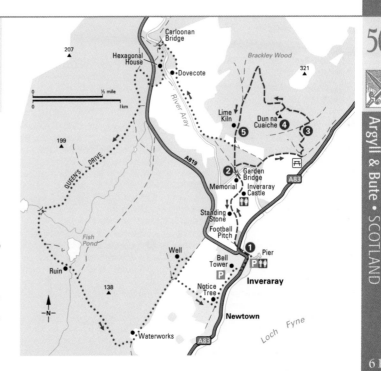

STIRLING A Braveheart

Discover the truth about William Wallace on this town trail.

5 miles/8km 2hrs 30 min **Ascent** 279ft/85m ⚠ **Difficulty** 1

Paths Ancient city streets and some rough tracks

Map OS Explorer 366 Stirling & Ochil Hills West **Grid ref** NS 795933

Parking On streets near TIC or in multi-storey car parks

❶ From TIC on Dumbarton Road, cross road and turn **L**. Walk past statue of Robert Burns then, before Albert Halls, turn **R** and walk retrace steps. Past statue of Rob Roy, turn **L** and take path along Back Wall.

❷ Soon turn **R** up steps tto Upper Back Wall. It's a steady climb, up past Church of Holy Rude, where James VI was crowned in 1567 and on past Ladies' Rock – where castle ladies sat to watch tournaments.

❸ Continue uphill to reach Stirling Castle. Cross car park to take path running downhill to just side of visitor centre, so that castle is on **L**. At cemetery, turn **R** along footpath signposted to Moto Hill. Continue up steps and across cemetery to gap in wall.

❹ Follow track downhill on to Gowan Hill. There are branching tracks but continue on main path – heading for cannons on hill ahead. At junction turn **R** down track signposted to Lower Bridge Street. Turn on to grassy slope to **R** to see Beheading Stone. Retrace your steps to wide track and then follow it to reach road.

❺ Turn **R** along Lower Bridge Street, then fork **R** into Upper Bridge Street. Continue ahead, then 50yds (46m) beyond Settle Inn, turn **R** up cobbled lane (it looks a bit like access to house). Follow it uphill, then go **L** at top. Eventually you pass Castle Esplanade, followed by Argyll's Lodging, and will reach junction.

❻ Turn **L**, passing Hermann's Restaurant and Mercat Cross. Turn **R** at bottom down Bow Street, then **L** on Baker Street. When you reach Friars Street (which is pedestrianised), turn **L** and walk down to end.

❼ Turn **R** now, then first **L** to station. Turn **L**, then **R** over bridge, then bear **L** in front of new development to reach riverside. Maintain direction and join Abbey Road. Bear **L** at end, go **R** over footbridge and continue along South Street, turning **R** at end to visit remains of Cambuskenneth Abbey.

❽ Retrace steps to station. Turn **R**, then **L**, then **R** again at Thistle Shopping Centre. Go along Port Street, then turn **R** along Dumbarton Road to start.

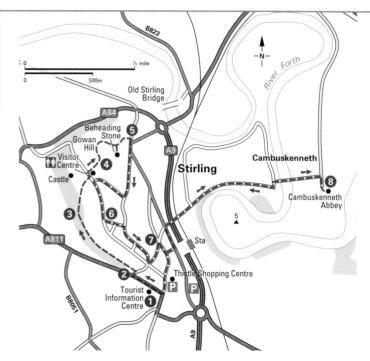

CALLANDER Romance Of Rob Roy

Steep wooded paths lead through the crags for views of the Trossachs.

4 miles/6.4km 2hrs 30min **Ascent** 896ft/273m ⚠ **Difficulty** ③
Paths Forest tracks and some rocky paths
Map OS Explorer 365 The Trossachs **Grid ref** NN 625079 **Parking** Riverside car park

❶ From Riverside car park, walk back to main road, then turn **L**. Follow this, then turn **R** along Tulipan Crescent. In front of modern flats, turn **L** and follow wide track. Where track splits, take path on **L**, signposted 'The Crags'.

❷ Path now winds steeply uphill through trees and can get slippery if there's been rain. Continue and cross footbridge. Climb to reach wall on **L-H** side, after which path narrows. Follow it to pass large boulder.

❸ Continue on path, which eventually bears **L**, up steps to fence. Cross another footbridge, scramble over rocks and go through metal kissing gate. You eventually reach memorial cairn, created in 1897 for Queen Victoria's Diamond Jubilee. On a clear day there are stunning, panoramic views of the surrounding countryside from here.

❹ Leaving cairn, path now begins to wind downhill. It's rocky in places so take. Follow path down to road.

❺ Turn **R** along road – Wallace Monument near Stirling is in far distance. Soon pass sign on the **R-H**

side for Red Well, where water runs a distinctly reddish colour owing to the presence of iron traces in the rock. Continue to car park on **L**. You can make a detour here to see Bracklyn Falls.

❻ After car park, stay on road for about 0.25 mile (400m) passing track up to reservoir on **R**, then turn **R** into Forestry Commission car park (signposted 'The Crags').

❼ Continue to walk through car park on to a broad Forestry Commission track. Continue walking past telecommunications next to the end of the track. At track end, turn **L** and then walk downhill to wooden seat and footbridge.

❽ Take path running **R** of seat (don't cross footbridge). Follow path as it runs downhill and back to place at it entered woods. Turn **R**, then go **L** along main road and walk back into Callander to car park at start of walk.

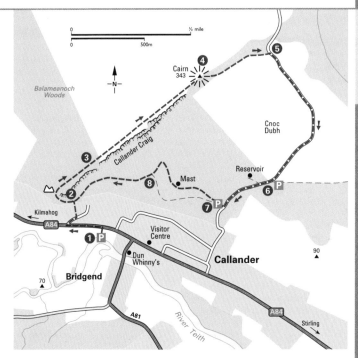

THE WHANGIE A Gash In The Rock

The hidden training ground of generations of rock climbers.

2.5 miles/4km 3hrs **Ascent** 515ft/157m ⚠ **Difficulty** 2
Paths Hill tracks and well-trodden footpaths, 2 stiles
Map OS Explorer 347 Loch Lomond South **Grid ref** NS 511808s
Parking Queen's View car park

❶ Head toward **L** of car park on to a small hillock where Queen Victoria stood for her first breathtaking view of Loch Lomond. Descend and cross stile over wall where well-defined path crosses duckboards and meanders uphill. Turn **R** to follow edge of wood. After duckboards this is pleasant grassy walk.

❷ At top, near fence, admire view. Look away to **R** for Loch Lomond, Ben Lomond towering over it to **R** and the Arrochar Hills away **L**. Cross ladder stile by tumbledown fence and turn **R** on to narrow but well-trodden path. Follow this along side of hill.

❸ When path forks go **L** and head uphill. Near top see Ordnance Survey pillar on summit of Auchineden Hill. Head to this on clear path. The ground is often boggy and you may have to leave path to bypass worst bits. To south from here are Kilpatrick Hills and, beyond them, River Clyde. Look for Burncrooks Reservoir to **R** and Kilmannan Reservoir to **L**. Beyond that is Cochno Loch, another reservoir, a favourite excursion for residents of nearby Clydebank.

❹ Looking towards Ben Lomond, the area in front is Stockie Muir, where the Devil was heading for the tryst that created the Whangie. Walk towards Ben on path leading away from Ordnance Survey pillar and go downhill into dip. Another path runs across. Turn **L** on to it and follow it round side of small hill. Where path curves **R**, look for crags on **R**.

❺ Here is hidden opening to the Whangie. It's easy to miss; look for spot on **R** where it is simple to climb few steps up to crags. Wall seems to open up. Climb into Whangie and walk to other end on path.

❻ Exit the Whangie and head to **R** on another footpath. Continue until it rejoins path of uphill journey. Go back to stile then retrace steps downhill and back to car park.

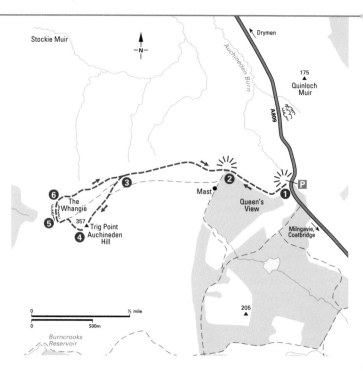

ABERFOYLE Queen Elizabeth Forest Park

The Highland Boundary Fault and along a 19th-century inclined railway.

4 miles/6.4km 3hrs **Ascent** 446ft/136m △ **Difficulty** 2
Paths Forest roads and footpaths
Map OS Explorer 365 The Trossachs **Grid ref** NN 519014
Parking At visitor centre near Aberfoyle

1 From front of visitor centre turn **L**, go down steps on to well-surfaced footpath and turn **L** to follow blue waymarkers of Highland Boundary Fault Trail. Continue on trail to reach Waterfall of the Little Fawn with its 55ft (16.7m) drop. Shortly after turn **L** to cross bridge, then turn **R** following white arrow **L** again on to forest road.

2 This is part of National Cycle Network (NCN) so look out for cyclists. Head uphill on this waymarked road following blue Highland Boundary Fault markers and NCN Route 7 signs. When road forks at junction, keep L continuing uphill to crossroads.

3 Turn **R**, at blue waymarker, on to smaller and rougher road. Boundary Fault Trail parts company with NCN Route 7 here. Going is easy along this fairly level section. Continue until you reach viewpoint on the **R**.

4 From here road heads uphill until it reaches waymarker near path heading uphill towards mast. Turn **R** then go through barrier and start descending. This is well-made path but very steep descent through

the woods and great care should be taken.

5 Path follows line of Limecraigs Railway, an early 19th-century inclined railway used for transporting limestone. It continues downhill to go through another barrier where path is intersected by forest road. Cross road, go through another barrier and once again continue downhill.

6 At bottom of hill steps lead to forest road. Turn **R** on to road and follow blue waymarkers. Stay on road until you reach green signpost on **L** pointing to visitor centre. Turn **L** on to downhill track and head through woods.

7 Eventually you'll reach board announcing trail end. From here route is signed back to visitor centre. When trail forks take **R-H** turning and head uphill beside handrail and return to start.

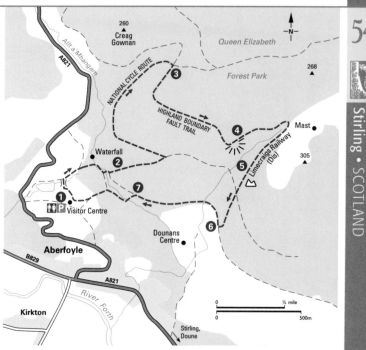

ABERFOYLE Great Forest Of Ard

Discover the Stone of Destiny's hiding place and birthplace of the Scottish Parliament.

3.5 miles/5.7km 2hrs **Ascent** 98ft/30m ⚠ **Difficulty** ☐
Paths Roads, forest roads and trails
Map OS Explorer 365 The Trossachs **Grid ref** NS 521009
Parking Car park at Aberfoyle beside tourist office in centre of town

① Leave from west end of car park and turn **L** into Manse Road. Cross narrow bridge over River Forth (river has its source near here) and continue along grass beside road until first junction on **R**. Turn **R** here and head uphill, passing Covenanters' Inn. A short distance past here is open countryside and start of Great Forest of Loch Ard.

② Head straight on along forest road, keeping an ear open for heavy timber lorries. During the week this can get fairly busy, as this is a main forestry extraction route, so keep well into the side. After about 0.5 mile (800m) you will reach staggered crossroads. Continue straight ahead along forest road until you come to turning on **R** with yellow waymarker. Turn **R**.

③ Follow this waymarked trail through forest almost to banks of Duchray Water. This rises on north face of Ben Lomond and joins with Avondhu from Loch Ard to create River Forth near Aberfoyle. Path now curves **R**, continues to descend slightly and then reaches junction.

④ Turn **R** and follow path through trees to north banks of Lochan Spling. Path then swings **L** and, at end of Lochan, turns **R** at waymarker pole, crosses small stream and heads slightly uphill.

⑤ When path reaches T-junction, turn **L** and rejoin main forest access road continuing to Covenanters' Inn. This takes its name not from the activities of the 17th-century Scottish Presbyterians, who were persecuted by the Stuart monarchy for refusing to give up their faith, but from the subsequent activities of 20th-century Scottish Nationalists.

⑥ Continue past inn, where a later group of Nationalists temporarily hid Scotland's Stone of Destiny when it was liberated from Westminster Abbey in 1950, and then turn **L** on to Manse Road at junction and return back to start.

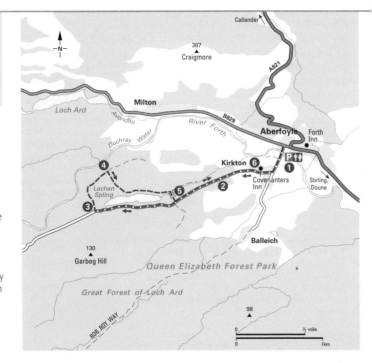

LOCH LOMOND The Sallochy Woods

A gentle stroll by the bonnie banks of Loch Lomond, Britain's largest freshwater lake.

2 miles/3.2km 1hr 30min **Ascent** 131ft/40m ⚠ **Difficulty** 1️⃣
Paths West Highland Way, forest trail and forest road
Map OS Explorer 364 Loch Lomond North **Grid ref** NS 380957
Parking Sallochy Woods car park

❶ From car park head towards entrance on to main road. Go **R** on to track beside starting post to Sallochy Trail. Cross road with care and continue along trail on other side. Follow red, green and blue waymarkers. At second junction turn **R** and follow green waymarkers.
❷ Trail goes through wood and passes into ruined 19th-century farm steading of Wester Sallochy which Forestry Commission has now cleared of trees. Several buildings can be seen and it's worth spending some time investigating these old ruins and trying to imagine life in those times. When you have finished, circle buildings to **L** and follow well-worn trail until it ends at T-junction beside waymarker post. Turn **R** on to forest road here.
❸ Follow forest road for about 0.5 mile (800m) to reach gate just before junction with main road. Through gate, then cross main road. Look carefully for faint path running through woods to **L**.
❹ Follow faint path back towards loch (if you miss track then enter wood at any point and head west

towards loch). When track intersects with well-surfaced footpath, turn **R**. You are now on West Highland Way. Follow waymarkers, keeping on main path and ignoring any subsidiary tracks branching off.
❺ Follow path uphill through rocky section and then, as it levels off, through wood. Eventually trail passes through Sallochy Woods car park returning to start.

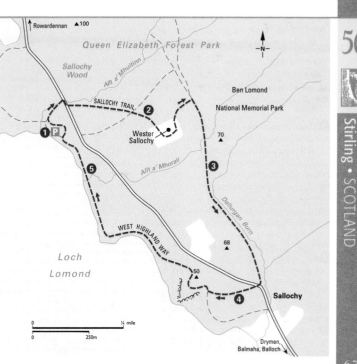

BALQUHIDDER On The Trail Of An Outlaw

Follow the trail of the Highland outlaw, Rob Roy, and on to see his final resting place.

2.5 miles/4km 2hrs **Ascent** 328ft/100m ⚠ **Difficulty** 2
Paths Forest roads and hillside, 2 stiles
Map OS Explorer 365 The Trossachs **Grid ref** NN 536209
Parking At Balquhidder church

❶ Walk starts at car park at Balquhidder church. From here, walk along dirt track, go past shed and turn on to path on **R-H** side which gives access into forest. Follow direction arrows on green signposts pointing to Creag an Tuirc, along forest track and heading up hill.

❷ Continue on this obvious trail for about 0.5 mile (800m) and then turn **R**, alongside green building, again following clearly signposted and waymarked route along forest road. After another 0.5 mile (800m) go through gate on **R**, go slightly downhill on stone steps and cross small stream.

❸ Path now heads uphill on stone steps, through old pine trees and on towards summit of knoll. Here is a cairn erected by the Clan Maclaren Society in 1987 to commemorate their 25th anniversary. The plaque proclaims that this place is the ancient rallying point of their clan.

❹ A seat below the cairn is a grand place to rest after the climb up here. Sit for a while and enjoy the magnificent views. You can see the route that Rob Roy's funeral procession would have taken from Inverlochlarig down to the village itself, and the churchyard where his body lies. From here, retrace your steps back down hill but before reaching top of stone steps on which you came up, take path to the **L** signposted 'Forest Walk'. This continues downhill following waymarked poles, down steps and across small bridge. Path goes through some bracken, over small stream and then across stile. Eventually it passes through small wood of young native trees before emerging on to forest road.

❺ Turn **L** here and retrace your steps back downhill over stile and then turn **L** to return to car park. From here enter churchyard and turn **L**. Rob Roy's grave is on **L** in front of ruins of pre-Reformation church.

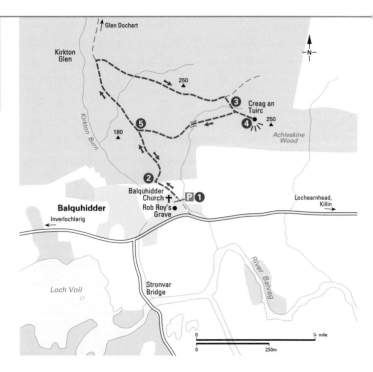

LOCH KATRINE Along The Shore

A walk around Glasgow's water supply in the heart of the Trossachs.

6.75 miles/10.9km 4hrs 30min **Ascent** 420ft/128m ⚠ **Difficulty** ②
Paths Water board roads, hill tracks
Map OS Explorers 364 Loch Lomond North; 365 The Trossachs **Grid ref** NN 404102 (on Explorer 364)
Parking Car park at Stronachlachar Pier

❶ From car park follow road back towards B829 and take second turning on **L**. This is an access road for Scottish Water vehicles only. Continue along access road until you come to cattle grid with green gate posts at building known as Royal Cottage. Turn **R** just before this on to rough gravel track that heads through some dense bracken.

❷ As path emerges on to open hillside you see first of several ventilation shafts and beyond it, on hill, strange obelisk. Follow path along this line. At obelisk be sure to look back for a magnificent view over Loch Katrine below and across to the hills with their narrow passes. This is where Rob Roy and his men moved from Loch Katrine to Balquhidder and beyond, moving cattle or escaping from the forces of law and order. Continue following line of ventilation shafts towards chimney-like structure on top of hill. Skirt this hill to **R** and then continue around its **L-H** side, following obvious forestry track.

❸ Follow this well-defined track past another ventilation shaft. Keep **L** at shaft. It can be very muddy on this short stretch. Continue on path until it intersects forest road by stream. Cross road and look for faint track continuing downhill in same direction. In summer path may be difficult to find because it's hidden by bracken. In this case follow line of telephone poles. Eventually after working downhill through more woodland track emerges on to B829.

❹ Turn **R** here and follow road. It will eventually emerge from Loch Ard Forest into open countryside. Loch Arklet can be seen on **L**; it is now connected to Loch Katrine by underground pipeline. When road reaches T-junction with Inversnaid road, turn **R**. When road forks, turn **R** again and return to Stronachlachar Pier.

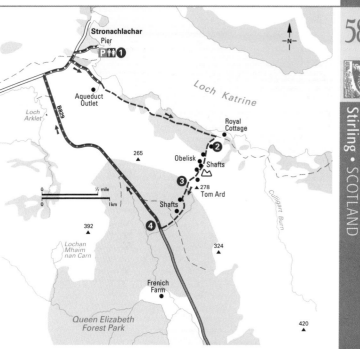

CARBETH The Hut Community
Discover a working-class Utopian dream.

3 miles/4.8km 2hrs 30min **Ascent** 98ft/30m ⚠ **Difficulty** ☐1
Paths Roads, access tracks and footpaths, 1 stile
Map OS Explorer 348 Campsie Fells **Grid ref** NX 524791
Parking Carbeth Inn, check beforehand with landlord

❶ From Carbeth Inn car park turn **R** on to A809. After 0.25 mile (400m) take first turning **R** on to B821. Continue on this road for 1 mile (1.6km), passing collection of huts on **L** ignoring public footpath sign **R**.
❷ Turn **R** at signpost for West Highland Way. There's also Scottish Rights of Way Society signpost beside this pointing to Khyber Pass Road to Mugdock Country Park. This was the favoured route of the early walkers heading out of Glasgow to the Campsie Fells and beyond.
❸ Go through gate and continue along well-surfaced access road. Ignoring Khyber Pass turn-off, keep **R** to follow West Highland Way along access road to more huts. After passing first of huts and reaching **L** bend in path, look out for partially concealed public path signpost on **R** beside West Highland Way marker post.
❹ Turn **R** here on to narrow but well-surfaced footpath and continue along it, passing Carbeth Loch on **R-H** side, to reach junction with drive leading to Carbeth House. This is a private house and is not open

to the public. Turn **L**, pass house and huts on **R** then take next turning on **L**.
❺ Continue along lane, then head uphill to reach another grouping of Carbeth huts. Follow main route through huts and when it forks, keep **L**.
❻ Keep on road as it passes through main part of Carbeth huts, an extraordinary assortment of small dwellings, shanties and shacks. Ignore all smaller tracks branching off road. They allow access to individual huts or other parts of settlement.
❼ Eventually reach T-junction. Turn **R** and follow lane as it winds downhill to reach junction with A809 beside Carbeth Inn. Turn **L** and return to car park.

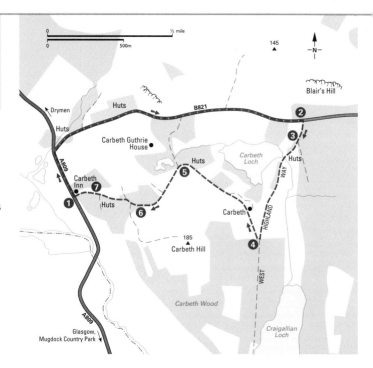

CULROSS A Leisurely Circuit

An easy walk around an historic town.

3.5 miles/5.7km 1hr 30min **Ascent** 180ft/55m ⚠ **Difficulty** 1
Paths Generally firm paths, some muddy woodland tracks
Map OS Explorer 367 Dunfermline & Kirkcaldy **Grid ref** NS 983859
Parking Culross West car park

❶ From car park, take steps up to tarmac path alongside railway and turn **R**. Just beyond reed bed to **R**, turn **R** down steps and follow path to road. Cross over to entrance to Blair Castle, now convalescent home for miners.

❷ Walk up tarmac drive, which is lined with magnificent rhododendron bushes. Walk ahead until you see Blair Castle on **L**. Before you reach it, take **R-H** turning in trees and follow it as it bears to **R**. Continue to Blair Mains farmhouse, on **L**.

❸ Continue following track, with fields on either side. Walk ahead to trees and continue following track until you reach metal gate on **L-H** side, just beyond line of pylons. Look carefully and you should spot a wooden fence post on **R-H** side, with words 'West Kirk' and 'grave' painted on it in faint white. Take narrow **R-H** path immediately before it, which runs through trees.

❹ Follow path to go through kissing gate and continue walking ahead, with trees on **L** and fields on **R**. Go through another kissing gate, and continue in

same direction. When you reach crossing of paths, continue ahead along track and walk under line of pylons. You will soon pass remains of church on **L**.

❺ Continue ahead, past old cemetery, and walk in same direction until track joins tarmac road. Walk in same direction to junction. Turn **R** and head downhill – watch for traffic now as road can be busy. You will soon reach Culross Abbey on **L**.

❻ It's worth stopping to visit abbey. Then continue to walk downhill, down Tanhouse Brae, to soon reach Mercat ('old Market') Cross, with The Study on **R**. Continue walking in same direction, down Back Causeway, to main road.

❼ Turn **R**, walk past tourist information centre, past Tron (old burgh weighing machine), then past large ochre-coloured building on **R**, which is Culross Palace. To reach starting point, continue walking in same direction –car park is on **L**, just past play area.

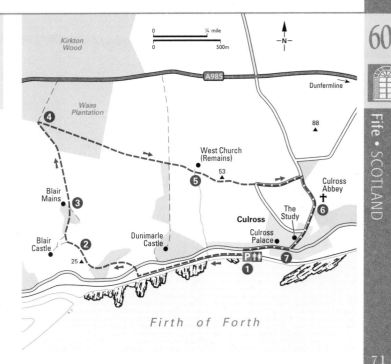

ST ANDREWS Academic Traditions

A town trail to an ancient monument.

4.5 miles/7.2km 2hrs **Ascent** 33ft10m ⚠ **Difficulty** ☐1

Paths Ancient streets and golden sands **Map** OS Explorer 371 St Andrews & East Fife

Grid ref NO 506170 **Parking** Free parking along The Scores, otherwise several car parks

❶ With Martyrs Monument on The Scores in front of you, walk **L** past bandstand. At road turn **R**, walk to British Golf Museum, then turn **L**. Pass clubhouse of Royal and Ancient Golf Club on **L**, then bear **R** at burn to reach beach.

❷ Route now goes along West Sands. Walk as far as you choose, then either retrace your steps along beach or take any path through dunes to join tarmac road. Walk back to Golf Museum, then turn **R** and walk to main road.

❸ Turn **L** along road and walk to St Salvator's College. Peek through archway at serene quadrangle – and look at initials PH in cobbles outside. They commemorate Patrick Hamilton, who was martyred here in 1528 – they say students who tread on the site will fail their exams. Cross over and walk to end of College Street.

❹ Turn **R** and walk along Market Street. At corner turn **L** along Bell Street, then **L** again on South Street. Opposite Holy Trinity Church, turn R down Queens

Gardens to reach Queens Terrace.

❺ Turn **R** then immediately **L** down steeply sloping Dempster Terrace. At end cross burn, turn **L** and walk to main road. Cross and walk along Glebe Road. At park, take path that bears **L**, walk past play area and up to Woodburn Terrace.

❻ Turn **L** to join St Mary Street and cross main road to follow Woodburn Place down towards beach. Just before slipway, turn **L** along tarmac path. Cross footbridge and join road.

❼ Bear **R** for few paces, then ascend steps on **L** to the remains of a church and famous ruined cathedral. Gate in wall on **L** gives access to site.

❽ Route then follows beachfront past ancient castle on **R**, a former palace/fortress. Pass Castle Visitor Centre, then continue along The Scores to return to start.

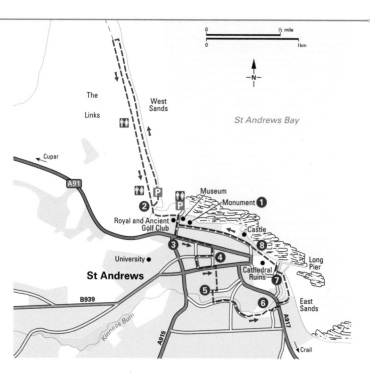

EAST NEUK A Fishy Trail

A linear coastal walk through East Neuk.

4 miles/6.4km 1hr 30min **Ascent** 49ft/15m ⚠ **Difficulty** 1

Paths Well-marked coastal path, 3 stiles
Map OS Explorer 371 St Andrews & East Fife **Grid ref Start** NO 613077 **Finish** NO 569034
Parking On street in Crail

❶ From tourist information centre, walk down Tolbooth Wynd. At end turn **R**; where road divides, bear **L** (signed 'no vehicular access to harbour'). Now walk beside old castle wall to lookout point for view of harbour. Bear **R** and walk on to High Street.
❷ Turn **L** and walk along road out of village, passing 2 white beacons, which help guide boats into harbour. Turn **L** and walk down West Braes, following signs for Coastal Path. When you reach Osbourne Terrace turn **L** down narrow path, then descend steps, through kissing gate and on to grassy track by shore.
❸ Follow path as it hugs shoreline. You should soon see cormorants perched on rocks to **L** and will also get views of Isle of May. Go down steps, over slightly boggy area, and continue walking to 2 derelict cottages – area known as The Pans.
❹ Pass cottages and continue along shore, then cross stone stile. Pass flat rocks on **L**. Cross burn by footbridge –Bass Rock and Berwick Law are **L** and village of Anstruther ahead. Soon reach caves.

❺ Pass caves, then cross little stone stile on **L** and cross footbridge. Track is narrower and goes past fields on **R**, then maritime grasses on **L**. Stone steps lead to another stile. Cross to reach Caiplie.
❻ Go through kissing gate; pass in front of houses, follow grassy track; go through kissing gate to pass field. Path runs past pig farm and up to caravan park.
❼ Continue along shore, on tarmac track to reach play area and war memorial on **R**. Maintain direction as you enter village of Cellardyke and continue to harbour. Pass harbour and The Haven restaurant and continue along John Street, then James Street.
❽ At end of James Street maintain direction, then follow road as it bends down to **L**. Walk past guiding beacon to Anstruther's busy harbour. Either walk back to Crail or take bus from harbour.

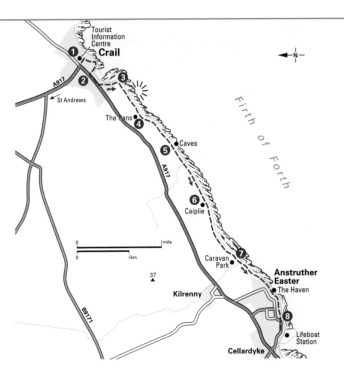

PERTH Along The Tay To Scone

A town trail around Perth with views over Scotland's ancient capital.

4 miles/6.4km 2hrs **Ascent** Negligible ⚠ **Difficulty** 1
Paths City streets and wide firm tracks
Map OS Explorer 369 Perth & Kinross **Grid ref** NO 114237
Parking On street in Perth

❶ From tourist information centre turn **R**, then take the first **R** to walk round building. Turn **R** again and walk down to road. Cross into Murray Street, passing bus stops and continue across Kinnoul Street into Mill Street.

❷ Continue down Mill Street, passing Perth Theatre on **R-H** side. Keep walking ahead, pass Caffe Canto on **R**, and join Bridge Lane. Pass museum and art gallery on **L** and come on to Charlotte Street. Turn **L**.

❸ At corner turn **L** to visit Fair Maid's House. Otherwise, cross road and turn **R** through park. Walk past statue of Prince Albert then bear **L** to join riverside path. This gives good views of smart houses along opposite bank.

❹ Continue on path, passing golf course. At sign for 14th tee, turn **R** and follow track, with wall to **L** at water's edge. Either follow cycle track to **L** of wall, or walk along river bank.

❺ Follow chosen track until 2 tracks meet, just past electricity substation. Walk by riverside now to enjoy great views of Scone Palace on opposite bank. This is a lovely spot on a warm, summer's day.

❻ Retrace steps, walking back beside river or along cycle track and back to golf course. Turn **L** and walk back towards Perth to cricket and football pitches on **R**.

❼ Turn **R** and walk between pitches to join Rose Terrace –John Ruskin lived here. Turn **L**, then bear **L** at end into Charlotte Street and **R** into George Street, then **R** again into Bridge Lane. Turn **L** along Skinner Gate, site of oldest pub in Perth, and walk along to end.

❽ Cross to pass around St John Kirk, through archway into South Street and across Princes Street. At Marshall Place turn **L** and head to Fergusson Gallery on **L-H** side. Turn back along Marshall Place, walk up to King Street and then turn **R**. Maintain direction now, then turn **L** into West Mill Street and return to start.

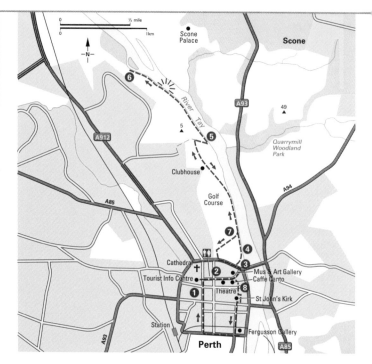

FORTINGALL An Ancient Yew

An easy walk amid mountain scenery.

3.5 miles/5.6km 2hrs **Ascent** 33ft/10m ⚠ **Difficulty** ☐
Paths Quiet roads and firm farm tracks, 1 stile
Map OS Explorer 378 Ben Lawers & Glen Lyon **Grid ref** NN 741470
Parking Fortingall village

❶ With your back to Fortingall Hotel, turn **R** along road, passing several pretty thatched cottages (unusual in Scotland) on **R-H** side. Follow road over burn and then past entrance to Glen Lyon farm. Eventually reach fork in road.

❷ Ignore **R-H** fork and maintain direction. Road soon crosses bridge over River Lyon.

❸ Cross bridge and continue on road (it's tarmacked but quiet), and pass little cottages on **R**. Continue to sign for Duneaves.

❹ Turn **L** and follow road – river is on **L-H** side. You feel as if you're in a secret valley as you walk along here, and in late summer you can pick wild raspberries by the roadside. Continue past area of woodland, after which you get views across valley to Fortingall.

❺ Continue on road until you see white house on **R-H** side. Leave metalled track and turn **L** 50yds (46m) before house, down track signposted to Duneaves Farmhouse – good views of surrounding hills.

❻ Follow wide, stony track down to Duneaves. Just before farmhouse go through gate in wall on **R-H** side. Then turn **L**, following path around fields and along river bank to rather bouncy footbridge. Bear **R** after crossing bridge, then continue through gate and join road.

❼ Turn **L** and walk back along road. Soon pass 2 sets of standing stones in field on **L** – six stones in a ring near road, and three further away. Walk back into Fortingall to reach starting place.

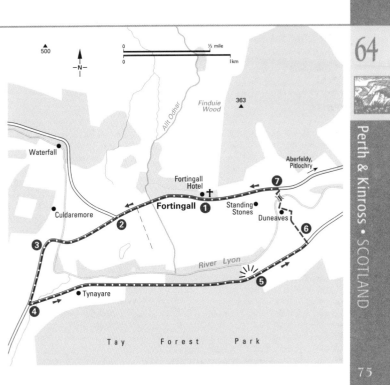

ALYTH The Sweet Fruits
Through the fertile heart of Scotland.

5 miles/8km 3hrs **Ascent** 787ft/240m ⚠ **Difficulty** 2
Paths Wide grassy tracks, some rougher paths on hill
Map OS Explorer 381 Blairgowrie, Kirriemuir & Glamis **Grid ref** NO 236486
Parking Car park in Alyth Market Square

❶ From Market Square, cross burn, then turn **L** along Commercial Street, so that river is on **L**. Turn **R** up Toutie Street, **R** again up Hill Street, then **L** on Loyal Road. Continue uphill to reach Cateran Trail sign.
❷ Walk uphill now, go through gate and continue in same direction, walking past wood on **R-H** side. Go through kissing gate, passing area that in summer is mass of purple foxgloves. Eventually path levels and then starts to bear downhill. Maintain direction to go through kissing gate and over burn.
❸ From here path becomes narrower and bears uphill again, becoming muddier and more overgrown. Walk under trees now, through gate, and then leave birch and oak woodland. Keep an eye out for deer here, as you might spot one bounding into the trees, just a few feet away from. Maintain direction through grass, then go through kissing gate to reach road.
❹ Turn **L** along road, following signs to Hill of Alyth Walk. It's quiet along here, so you should meet few cars. Road passes conifer plantation, house on **R-H**

side and crosses cattle grid. Soon after, you turn **L** and follow signs for Cateran Trail.
❺ Walk uphill and, at a crossing of tracks, turn **R**. Then, within 50yds (46m), turn **L** uphill. At another crossing of paths, turn **R**. There are lots of paths traversing hill, so choose your own route here, but you must keep ponds on **L** and don't walk as far as beacon. At pond, bear **R** at waymark sign, aiming for small copse until you go through gate.
❻ Walk down along enclosed track – you'll see church spire below. At another track turn **L** and then **R** to continue downhill on metalled track. Walk under line of pylons and past farm to eventually reach village.
❼ Path now bears **L** along residential road and takes you downhill. Turn **R** and retrace steps along side of burn to the start at Market Square.

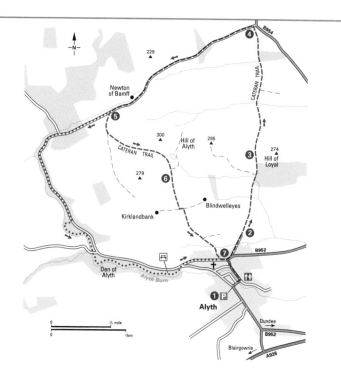

LOCH RANNOCH The Black Wood

In the ancient Caledonian forest.

3.75 miles/6km 2hrs 30min **Ascent** 1,150ft/350m ⚠ **Difficulty** ②
Paths Forest roads, rough woodland paths, no stiles
Map OS Explorer 385 Rannoch Moor & Ben Alder **Grid ref** NN 590567
Parking Small pull-in just west of Rannoch School

❶ From pull-in, walk back along road with Loch Rannoch on **L** and Rannoch School on **R**. Pass its commando climbing tower on **R**, sailing centre on **L** and golf course. At former school's goods entrance, Scottish Rights of Way Society (SRWS) signpost points up to **R** – old and unused through route to Glen Lyon. Follow tarred driveway past tennis courts to first buildings and turn **L** at another SRWS signpost.

❷ Sketchy path runs up under some fine birch trees. At empty gateway in decomposing fence it enters spruce trees and becomes narrow track that's damp in places. Avoid lesser path off to **L**; main one becomes pleasant green path contouring across slope with glimpses of Loch Rannoch on **R**. Path runs up to wide forest road.

❸ Ignore path continuing opposite and turn **R**, contouring around hill. Clear-felling has opened up views to Loch Rannoch and hills beyond. The highest of these, with a steep **R** edge, is Ben Alder, the centre of the southern Highlands. Hill is glimpsed from many places, notably A9 at Dalwhinnie, but isn't easily reached from anywhere. After 0.5 mile (800m), keep ahead where another track joins from **L**. Joined tracks descend to triangle junction. Turn **L**, gently uphill and, after 120yds (110m), bear **R** on to little-used old track. This descends to bridge across Dall Burn.

❹ Some 120yds (110m) after bridge, track bends **L**; here path descends on **R**. This is Black Wood of Rannoch, now forest reserve. Path runs under beautiful pines and birches. On **R**, Dall Burn is sometimes in sight and can always be heard. Path is quite rough, but unmistakable as it cuts through deep bilberry and heather. After 1 mile (1.6km), path bends **L** to track. Turn **R** to leave Caledonian Reserve at notice board. At T-junction, turn **L**, away from bridge leading into former school. Track improves as it runs past school's indoor swimming pool and back to lochside road.

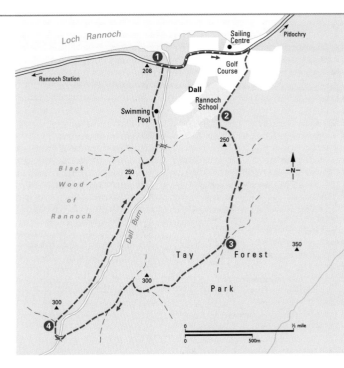

GLEN TILT A Royal Route

Following Queen Victoria's route through the Grampians.

6.5 miles/10.4km 3hrs 15min **Ascent** 852ft/250m ⚠ **Difficulty** ▣

Paths Estate tracks and smooth paths, 1 stile

Map OS Explorers 386 Pitlochry & Loch Tummel; 394 Atholl **Grid ref** NN 866662 (on Explorer 386)

Parking Blair Castle main car park **WARNING** Track goes through firing range and is closed on a few days each year. Consult Atholl Estate Ranger service

❶ Turn **R** in front of castle to 6-way signpost; bear **R** for gate into Diana's Grove. Bear **L** on wide path to Diana herself. Turn **R** on path to giant redwood tree and then bear **L**, to cross Banvie Burn on footbridge alongside road bridge. Soon gate leads to road.

❷ Now at Old Blair. Follow Minigaig Street ahead uphill. It eventually becomes track and enters forest. Ignore track on **L** and, in another 0.25 mile (400m), fork **R**. In 60yds (55m) pass path down to **R** with green waymarker. This is return route if firing range ahead is closed. Otherwise keep ahead to emerge from trees at firing range gate.

❸ Red flag flies if range is in use, but read notice carefully as on most firing days track through range may be used. Follow main track gently downhill, well below firing range targets, to riverside, then fork **R** to Gilbert's Bridge.

❹ Cross and turn **R** over cattle grid. Follow track for 220yds (201m), then turn **L** up steep path under trees to stile. Green track now runs down-valley along top of larch wood. Enter gate into birch wood, keep on main track, gently uphill. Gate leads to track, then road.

❺ Turn **R**, down long hill, crossing waterfalls. At foot of hill turn **R**, signed 'Old Blair', to cross Old Bridge of Tilt, then turn **L** into car park.

❻ To **R** of signboard, yellow waymarkers indicate path under trees to River Tilt. Turn **R** through exotic grotto until wooden steps on **R** lead up to corner of caravan park. Head away from river under pines. Ignore track on **R** and, at corner of caravan park, keep ahead under larch trees following faint path. Cross track to take big beech avenue towards Blair Castle. Bear **L** at statue of Hercules, passing Hercules Garden to front of castle.

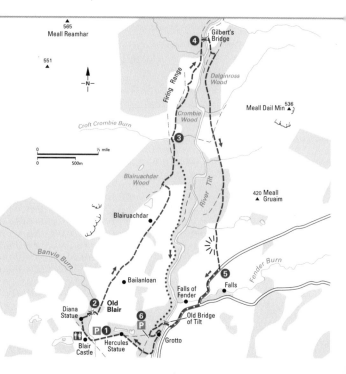

LOCH FASKALLY The Braes O' Killiecrankie
From the battlefield to Loch Faskally.

8.75 miles/14.1km 4hrs **Ascent** 492ft/150m ⚠ **Difficulty** ☐1☐
Paths Wide riverside paths, minor road, no stiles **Map** OS Explorer 386 Pitlochry & Loch Tummel
Grid ref NN 917626 **Parking** Killiecrankie visitor centre

❶ From back corner of visitor centre, steps signed 'Soldier's Leap' lead into wooded gorge. Footbridge crosses waterfall of Trouper's Den. At next junction, turn **L** ('Soldier's Leap'). Ten steps down, spur path **R** leads to viewpoint above Soldier's Leap.

❷ Return to main path, signed 'Linn of Tummel', which runs to River Garry below rail viaduct. After 1 mile (1.6km) path reaches footbridge.

❸ Don't cross footbridge; continue ahead, signed 'Pitlochry', along riverside under tall South Garry road bridge. Path bears **L** to footbridge. Cross, turn **R**, signed 'Pitlochry', to main river. Path runs around river pool to tarred lane; turn **R**. Lane leaves lochside, then passes track on **R**, blocked by vehicle barrier. Ignore track; shortly after turn **R** at signpost, 'Pitlochry'.

❹ Immediately bear **L** to pass along **R-H** side of Loch Dunmore, following red-top posts. Footbridge crosses loch, but turn away, half **R**, on to small path that becomes dirt track. After 270yds (250m) it reaches wider track. Turn **L**, with white/yellow waymarker. After

220yds (201m) track climbs; white/yellow markers indicate smaller path on **R**, which follows lochside to below A9 road bridge.

❺ Cross Loch Faskally on Clunie footbridge below road's bridge and turn **R**, on road around loch. In 1 mile (1.6km), at top of grass bank on **L**, is Priest Stone. Pass Clunie power station and reach car park on **L**. Sign indicates steep path down to Linn of Tummel.

❻ Return to road above for 0.5 mile (800m), to cross suspension bridge on **R**. Turn **R**, downstream, to pass above Linn. Spur path back **R** returns to falls at lower level, but main path continues along riverside (signed 'Killiecrankie'). It bends **L** and goes down wooden steps to Garry, then continues upstream and under high road bridge. Follow descending path signed 'Pitlochry via Faskally'. Path runs down to bridge, Point **❸**. Return upstream to start.

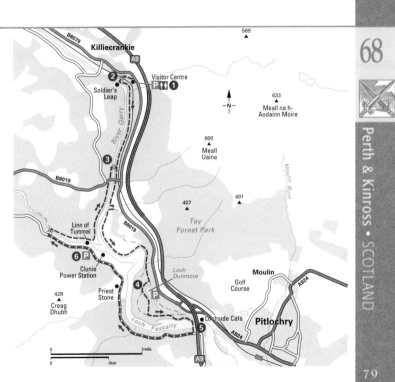

ABERLEMNO The Mysterious Stones

A lovely there-and-back route through a mysterious landscape once inhabited by the Picts.

5 miles/8km 1hr 45min **Ascent** 394ft/120m ⚠ **Difficulty** ②
Paths Mainly quiet roads but one extremely overgrown area
Map OS Explorer 389 Forfar, Brechin & Edzell **Grid ref** TQ 522558
Parking Car park by school in Aberlemno

❶ From car park, opposite Pictish stones, turn **R** and walk along road, then go first **L**, signed 'Aberlemno church and stone'. Walk past church – another Pictish stone is found in churchyard – and follow road as it bends round to **R**. Follow road until you reach T-junction.

❷ Turn **R** and follow this road, passing entrance to Woodside on **L**. At corner, follow road as it bends **R**. Walk down to join B9134, turn **R** and follow this short distance until you reach turning on **L**.

❸ Turn **L** along this road, signed 'Finavon Hill'. Road winds uphill, past several outcrops, then under line of pylons. Continue on road as it skirts hill.

❹ Continue following road uphill, passing small loch half-hidden in woodland to **L**. Shortly after, reach old stone wall on **R**. Just beyond rusty gate in corner of field, you see section of wall has collapsed. Hop over here, taking care to avoid strand of wire.

❺ Head uphill now to explore turf-covered ramparts of Finavon vitrified fort. Dating from the Iron Age

(1000 BC), the hilltop stronghold had walls built of stones that were fused together by tremendous heat. As you walk around summit, keep sharp eye out for vitrified material found in bank.

❻ From hilltop, return to road and turn **L** to retrace steps back to start of the walk in Aberlemno.

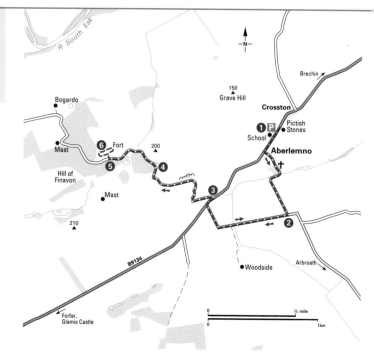

OLD ABERDEEN Striking Oil In The North Sea

This walk around the old fishing port celebrates the prosperity and tragedy that oil has brought to Aberdeen.

3.75 miles/6km 2hrs **Ascent** Negligible ⚠ **Difficulty** 1
Paths Mainly pavements; along beach (underwater at high tide)
Map OS Explorer 406 Aberdeen & Banchory **Grid ref** NJ 954067
Parking Esplanade at Fun Beach or Linx Ice Arena

❶ Head southwards on promenade, with sea on **L**. Go down slipway on to beach for short distance to wooden steps on **R** and leave beach to enter play area. (If tide is high at slipway: clamber over sea wall on **R**, and pass along row of fishermen's cottages.)

❷ Pass Silver Darling restaurant and head into harbour area. Continue past war memorial, keeping blue storage tanks to **L**, and along Pocra Quay as it bends **R**. Turn **L** into York Street and then at Neptune bar, turn **L** into York Place. Take first **R**, the first **L** and second **R** to emerge on Waterloo Quay.

❸ Where Waterloo Quay becomes Commerce Street, turn **L** into Regent Quay and then at T-junction cross dual carriageway at pedestrian lights. Turn **L** and then first **R** to reach Aberdeen Maritime Museum and John Ross's House. If you have time visit Maritime Museum.

❹ From here head along Exchequer Row, to turn **L** into Union Street. At once turn **R** into Broad Street, with Provost Skene's House on **L**, reached by passing underneath office block.

❺ Continue ahead past Marischal College (which houses the Marischal Museum), turn **R** into Littlejohn Street, and then cross North Street. At end of Meal Market Street turn **R** into King Street and then **L** into Frederick Street. At junction with Park Street turn **L** and go head until road crosses railway.

❻ Shortly after crossing is roundabout. Head slightly **R** along Park Road. Follow road through Trinity Cemetery and towards Pittodrie Park, home of Aberdeen Football Club, to junction with Golf Road.

❼ At junction with Golf Road, turn **R**, on well-made path over Broad Hill. There are wide views of sea and Aberdeen. At path end, turn **L** to roundabout with subtropical plants on Esplanade. Shoreline promenade leads back to start.

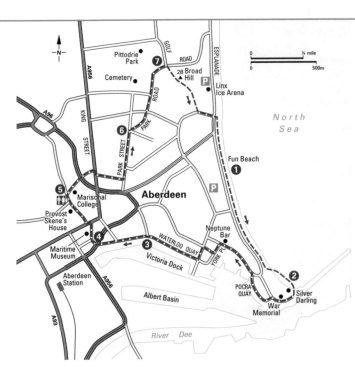

AUCHENBLAE An Inspirational Landscape
Walk through the Howe of Mearns.

6.75 miles/11km 3hrs 30min **Ascent** 459ft/140m ⚠ **Difficulty** 2

Paths Established footpaths, overgrown woodland tracks

Map OS Explorer 396 Stonehaven, Inverbervie & Lawrencekirk **Grid ref** NO 727787

Parking On street in Auchenblae

① Half-way up steep High Street, turn **L**, signed 'Woodland Walks'. Lane runs steeply downhill and crosses Pamphil Burn beside play area; then runs uphill to T-junction.

② Turn **R** past cemetery and then take grassy track on **L**. Track runs between fields to reach plantation above. Scramble over or past rusty gate (take care) and walk through long grass to reach track.

③ Turn **R** and follow thickly vegetated track along bottom edge of forest. Clamber over or walk around couple of fallen trees. At wider gravel track, turn **R** and continue with fields still visible through trees below. Above where fields end, ignore side-track up **L**. In another 220yds (200m), fork **L** on fainter track.

④ Track runs level then gently uphill. Where pylon rises on **R-H** side of track, strike downhill through cleared ground under electric wires –going is awkward, with brushwood underfoot.

⑤ At bottom **L** corner of cleared ground, path strikes **L** into forest. Path becomes clearer as it slants down to join valley road. Turn sharp **R** along road, passing huge Sitka spruce tree, to Drumtochty car park on **L**.

⑥ Take track through car park, bending up **L** past toilets. After stiff climb on tarmac, turn **R** (red waymarker) down zig-zag path to mill lade. Turn **L** along this, to footbridge above weir. Little way upstream, path climbs out of steep valley, and contours upstream to pass above small reservoir.

⑦ At track beyond, turn **L** and return to Drumtochty car park. Turn **L** along road until path forks up **R** past vehicle barrier to forest track, which joins larger one. Keep ahead until track descends **L** to rejoin road.

⑧ Turn **R** and walk along road, to junction to turn **L**, signed 'Auchenblae', and cross Pamphil Burn. At following junction bear **R**, to reach top end of Auchenblae's High Street.

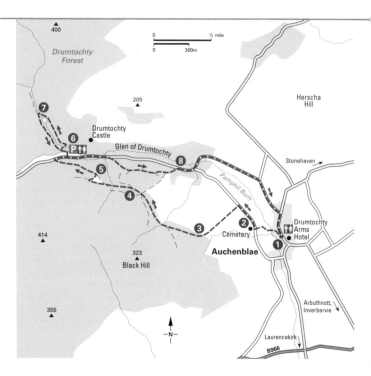

STONEHAVEN Hidden Treasure

Along the cliffs to Dunnottar Castle, which once housed Scotland's crown jewels.

3.5 miles/5.7km 1hr 30min **Ascent** 377ft/115m ⚠ **Difficulty** 1

Paths Cliff edges, metalled tracks, forest paths
Map OS Explorer 396 Stonehaven & Inverbervie **Grid ref** NO 874858
Parking Market Square, Stonehaven

1 From Market Square in Stonehaven, walk back on to Allardyce Street, turn **R** and cross road. Turn **L** up Market Lane and, at beach, turn **R** to cross footbridge. Turn **R** at sign to Dunnottar Castle to reach harbour. Cross here to continue down Shorehead, on east side of harbour. Pass Marine Hotel, turn **R** into Wallis Wynd.

2 Turn **L** into Castle Street. It becomes steep path, to emerge at main road, then maintain direction along the road until it bends. Continue ahead, following enclosed tarmac path, between arable fields and past war memorial **R-H** side. Cross middle of field, then above Strathlethan Bay.

3 Path turns **R** across middle of field and over footbridge. You now pass path going down to Castle Haven and continue following main path around cliff edge. Cross another footbridge and bear uphill. Soon reach steps on **L** that run down to Dunnottar Castle.

4 Your walk bears **R** here inland, past waterfall, through kissing gate and up to house. Pass house to road into Stonehaven by Dunnottar Mains, turn **R**, then take first turning **L**, to walk alongside farm. Follow wide, metalled track past East Newtonleys on the **L-H** side to main A957.

5 Turn **R** and go downhill, then take first road on **L** signed 'Dunnottar Church'. Follow this over Burn of Glaslow to path on **R** signed 'Carron Gate'. Take path into woods but at once fork **R**, following lower path that runs by burn. Continue to Shell House on **L**.

6 Just past Shell House, continue along lower path, which turns uphill to join higher path. Bear **R**, to reach end of woods at Carron Gate. Walk through housing estate to join Low Wood Road and River Carron.

7 Turn **L**, then **R** to cross footbridge with green railings. Turn **R** and walk by water. Soon pass striking art deco Carron Restaurant on **L**, and reach cream-coloured iron bridge. Bear **L** then turn first **R** to return to Market Square.

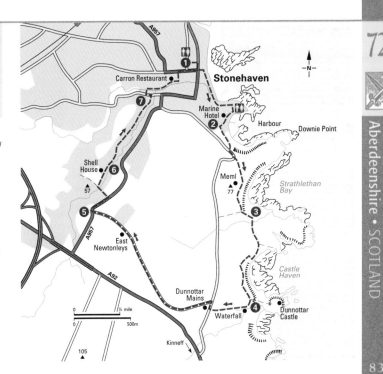

BRAEMAR Moorland On Morrone

The hill at the back of Braemar gives a taste of the Cairngorms.

6.75 miles/10.9km 4hrs 15min **Ascent** 2,000ft/608m ⚠ **Difficulty** ③

Paths Well-made but fairly steep path, track, 1 stile

Map OS Explorer 387 Glen Shee & Braemar **Grid ref** NO 143911

Parking Duck pond, at top of Chapel Brae, Braemar

❶ Take wide track uphill, to **R** of duck pond, bearing **L** twice following blue waymarkers to Woodhill house. House can be bypassed by taking small footpath on **R** which rejoins track just above. When track forks again, bear **L** to viewpoint indicator.

❷ Cross track diagonally to hill path marked 'Morrone'. Path has been rebuilt with rough stone steps. Higher up, it slants to **R** along line of rocky outcrops, a geological dyke of harder rock. At top it turns directly uphill, passing 5 sprawling cairns. These are turning point in the Morrone Hill Race – part of Braemar Games. Stony path runs up to radio mast.

❸ The summit, with your back on buildings, has views across the Cairngorms. On the main tops snow may show **R** through summer. To east are Loch Callater and White Mounth plateau. A notable hump is Cac Carn Beag, one of the summits of Lochnagar. Morrone's summit area is bare stones, but past buildings you'll find start of wide track. It runs down to shallow col and climbs to cairn on low summit

beyond. Here it bends **L** towards lower col, but before reaching it, turns **L** again down hillside. A gentle zig-zagging descent leads to road by Clunie Water.

❹ Turn **L**, alongside river, for 1.5 miles (2.4km). Ben Avon with its summit tors fills skyline ahead. After snow gate and golf clubhouse comes road sign warning of cattle grid (grid itself is round next bend). Here track, up to **L**, has blue-topped waymarker pole.

❺ Go up between caravans to ladder stile with dog flap. Faint path leads up under birches, bearing **R** and becoming clearer. After gate in fence path becomes clear, leading to Scottish Natural Heritage signboard and blue waymarker at top of birch wood. Path becomes track with fence on **R** and, in 220yds (201m), reaches viewpoint indicator, Point ❷. From here return to duck pond and start of walk.

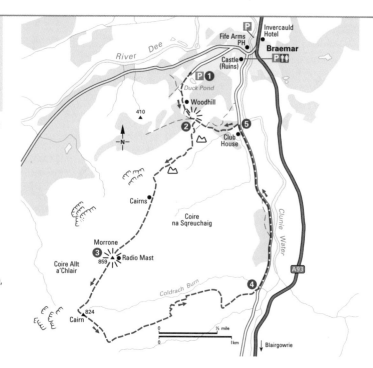

GLENLIVET The Whisky Hills

Through a green valley and heather moor.

6.25 miles/10.1km 3hrs 15min **Ascent** 1,000ft/305m ⚠ **Difficulty** ③
Paths Waymarked, muddy and indistinct in places, 11 stiles
Map OS Explorer 420 Correen Hills & Glenlivet **Grid ref** NJ 218257
Parking Track opposite church at Tombae runs up to quarry car park
WARNING Grouse shooting in August/September – consult Glenlivet Ranger Service at Tomintoul

❶ At Tombae church, turn **L** for 330yds (300m) to stile on **R** ('Walk 10'). Track leads down into woods. Bear **R** at waymarker and follow main track to reach bridge and cross River Livet. After 60yds (55m), turn **R** to another bridge, now over Crombie Water. Turn half **L**, up to stile beside field gate. Route follows top of low wooded bank above Crombie Water to footbridge (grid ref 226245).
❷ Across footbridge, small path runs across meadow into wood, slanting up to **R** to green track. Turn **R** and continue up through wood, then bend **L** on to heather moorland. Below abrupt hill of The Bochel track forks. Keep ahead, with waymarker. Way becomes peaty path. At top of 1st rise is stile with gate. Path, with waymarker, leads to gateway in another fence. Don't go through, but turn **R**, with fence on **L**, to stile with signpost.
❸ For easier alternative, follow sign for Walk 10, ahead. Just before house, turn **R** at another signpost and follow track towards Bochel farm. Main route goes over The Bochel itself. Across stile, turn uphill on sheep paths

to summit cairn. Turn **L**, to descend towards Braeval distillery below Ladder Hills. As slope steepens, see Bochel farm below. Head down **L-H** edge of nearer wood to join rough track leading into farm.
❹ At once gate on **R** leads to faint path into plantation. This soon becomes green track running just above bottom edge of wood. It becomes more well-used and then runs out to road.
❺ Turn **R**, over bridge to waymarked gate on **R**. Track rises to open fields above river. At its highest, waymarker points down to **R**. Go down to fence, with waymarked stile on **L**, then through heather with fence on your **L**. Turn downhill to stile at bottom. Cross this and turn **L**, ignoring another stile on **L**, to reach footbridge, Point ❷. Retrace first part of walk back to Tombae.

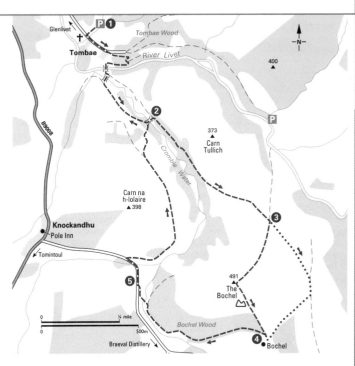

CORPACH The Banks Of The Caledonian Canal

A walk alongside and underneath Thomas Telford's masterpiece.

4.5 miles/7.2km 1hr 45min **Ascent** 100ft/30m ⚠ **Difficulty** ☐1

Paths Wide tow paths, no stiles

Map OS Explorer 392 Ben Nevis & Fort William **Grid ref** NN 097768

Parking Kilmallie Hall, Corpach

① Go down past Corpach Station to canal and cross sea lock that separates salt water from fresh water. Follow canal (on **L**) up past another lock, where path on **R** has blue cycle path sign and Great Glen Way marker. It passes under tall sycamores to shore. Follow shoreline path past football pitch and turn **L**, across damp grass to end of back street. Path ahead leads up wooded bank to tow path.

② Turn **R** along tow path, for 0.5 mile (800m). Just before Banavie swing bridge, path down to **R** has Great Glen Way marker. Follow waymarkers on street signs to level crossing, then turn **L** towards other swing bridge, with road on it.

③ Just before bridge, turn **R** Great Glen Way and Great Glen Cycle Route signs and continue along tow path to Neptune's Staircase. The 60ft (18m) of ascent alongside 8 locks is serious uphill walk, but more serious for boats. It takes about 90 minutes to work through the system.

④ Gate ends basin above locks. About 200yds (183m) later, grey gate on **R** leads to dump for dead cars; ignore this one. Just 220yds (200m) later canal crosses little wooded valley, with black fence on **R**. Now comes 2nd grey gate. Go through, to track turning back sharp **R** and descending to ford small stream.

⑤ On **R**, stream passes **R** under canal in arched tunnel, and alongside is 2nd tunnel, which provides walkers' way to other side. Water from canal drips into tunnel (it's a bit spooky) – try not to think of large boats sailing directly over your head! At tunnel's end, track runs up to join canal's northern tow path. Turn **R**, back down tow path. After passing Neptune's Staircase, cross A830 to level crossing without warning lights. Continue along the **R-H** tow path. After 1 mile (1.6km) tow path track leads back to Corpach double lock.

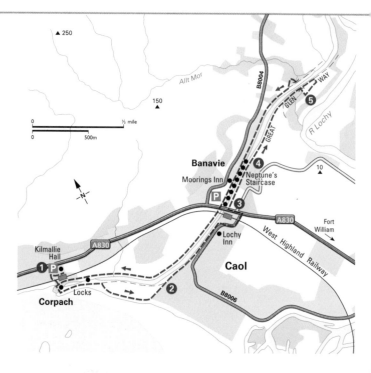

GRANTOWN-ON-SPEY Sir James Grant's Town

Around an 18th-century planned town.

7 miles/11.3km 3hrs **Ascent** 200ft/60m ⚠ **Difficulty** ☐1
Paths Tracks and smooth paths, 1 stile **Map** OS Explorer 419 Grantown-on-Spey **Grid ref** NJ 035280
Parking Grantown-on-Spey Museum

❶ Go down past museum. Turn **L** into South Street, then **R** into Golf Course Road. Tarred path crosses golf course to small gate into Anagach Wood.

❷ Wide path ahead has blue/red waymarker. At junction, blue trail departs to **R**; turn **L**, following Spey Way marker and red-top poles. Keep following red markers, turning **L** at 1st junction and bearing **L** at next. When track joins new fence and bend in stream is on **L**, keep ahead, following Spey Way marker.

❸ Track emerges into open fields. After crossing small bridge, turn **R** through new hunting gate. Path with pines on **L** leads to track near River Spey. (Bridge of Cromdale is just ahead.)

❹ Turn sharp **R** on track, alongside river. At fishers' hut it re-enters forest. About 0.75 mile (1.2km) later it diminishes to green path and slants up past cottage of Craigroy to join its entrance track.

❺ At Easter Anagach, grass track on **R** has red waymarkers and runs into birch wood. With barrier ahead, follow marker poles to **L**, on to broad path

beside falling fence. At next junction, turn **R**, following red poles, over slight rise. Descending, turn **L** just before blue-top post, on to smaller path with blue and red posts. This runs along ridge top, to reach bench above lane. To **L** down lane is handsome stone bridge built as part of military road system.

❻ Path bends **R**, alongside road, to meet wide track (former military road). Turn **R**, to path on **R** with green-top posts. At small pool, main path bends **L** for 150yds (137m), with blue and green posts; take path ahead, with green posts. A very old tree in the middle of the path was once used for public hangings. At five-way junction bear **L** to find next green post. At edge of golf course turn **L** to small car park and information board.

❼ Follow tarred street uphill, past end of golf course, to Grantown's High Street. Turn **R** to The Square. Just past Grant Arms Hotel, sign points **R**, to museum.

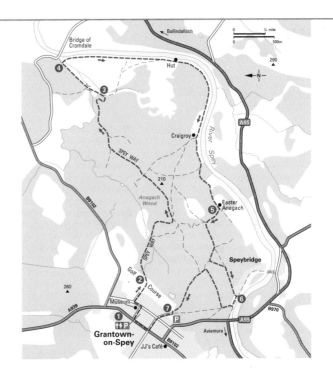

SHIELDAIG Loch-Side Shores

In the footsteps of Bonnie Prince Charlie around the inlets of the Shieldaig peninsula.

3.25 miles/5.3km 1hr 45min **Ascent** 500ft/152m ⚠ **Difficulty** 2
Paths Well-made old paths, 1 rough section **Map** OS Explorer 428 Kyle of Lochalsh
Grid ref NG 814538 **Parking** South end of Shieldaig village, opposite shop and hote

❶ Follow street along shoreline past cannon salvaged from Spanish Armada. At village end it rises slightly, with parking area, and war memorial above on **R**.
❷ In front of village school, turn **R** up a rough track. Track passes couple of houses to turn **L**. In another 100yds (91m) it divides; here main track for Rubha Lodge forks off **L**, but route bears **R**, passing to **R** of glacier-smoothed rock knoll. Terraced path runs through birch woods at first, with Loch Shieldaig below on **L**. It passes above 2 rocky bays, then strikes across peat bog, bright in mid-summer with bell heather and fluffy white tops of cotton grass. In middle of this flat area it divides at cairn.
❸ R-H path runs along edge of peaty area, with rocky ground above on **L**, then next to birch trees for 50yds (46m). Look for point where pink gravel surface becomes peaty, with rock formation like low ruin on **R**, because here is easily missed path junction.
❹ What seems like main footpath, ahead and slightly downhill, peters out eventually. Correct path forks off

to **L**, slanting up to higher ground just above. Path is now clear, crossing slabby ground in direction of peninsula's trig point, 0.25 mile (400m) away. After 220yds (201m) it rises slightly to gateway in former fence. Aiming **R** of trig point, it crosses small heather moor. At broken wall, path turns down **R** through gap to top of grassy meadow. First of 2 shoreline cottages, Bad-callda, is just below. Rough paths lead to **L** across boggy top of meadow and above birchwood, with trig point just above on **L**. Keep going forward at same level to heather knoll, with pole on it. Just below you is 2nd cottage, Camas-ruadh.
❺ Footpath zig-zags down to **R** between rocks. White paint spots lead round to **R** of cottage and shed. Turn **L** behind shed to join clear path coming from cottage. Return path is easy to follow, mostly along top of slope dropping to **R** to Loch Shieldaig. After 0.5 mile (800m) it rejoins outward route at cairn, Point ❸.

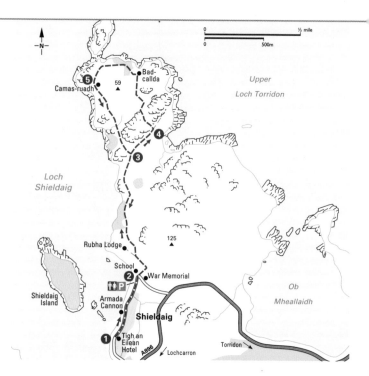

GLEN COE Into The Lost Valley
A rugged waterfall walk.

2.75 miles/4.4km 2hrs 15min **Ascent** 1,050ft/320m ⚠ **Difficulty** ③
Paths Rugged and stony, stream to wade through
Map OS Explorer 384 Glen Coe & Glen Etive **Grid ref** NN 168569
Parking Lower of two roadside parking places opposite Gearr Aonach (middle one of Three Sisters)

❶ From uphill corner of car park, faint path slants down to old road, now well-used wide path. Head up valley. With old road continuing as green track ahead, path now bends down to **R**. Path reaches gorge where River Coe runs in dyke of softer rock. Descend on a steep step ladder, to cross spectacular footbridge.
❷ Ascent out of gorge is on bare rock staircase. Above, path runs through regenerating birch wood, which can be wet on legs. Emerge through temporary fence by high gate. Path, rebuilt in places, runs uphill for 60yds (55m). Here it bends **L**; inconspicuous alternative path continues uphill, which bypasses narrow path of main route.
❸ Main route contours into Allt Coire Gabhail gorge. It is narrow with steep drops below. Where there is alternative of rock slabs and narrow path just below, slabs are more secure. Two fine waterfalls come into view. Pass these, continue between boulders to where main path bends **L** to cross stream below boulder size of small house. (Ignore small path which runs up **R** of

stream.) River here is wide and fairly shallow, 5 or 6 stepping stones usually allow dry crossing. If water is over stones, it's safer to wade alongside them; if water is more than knee-deep do not attempt crossing.
❹ Well-built path continues uphill, now with stream on **R**. After 100yds (91m) lump of rock blocks way. Path follows slanting ramp **R-H** side. It continues uphill, still rebuilt in places, passing above boulder pile that blocks valley, result of 2 rockfalls from under Gearr Aonach opposite. At top of rockpile path levels, giving view into Lost Valley.
❺ Drop gently to valley's gravel floor. Stream vanishes into gravel, to reappear below boulder pile on other side. Note where path arrives at gravel, as it becomes invisible at that point. Wander up valley to where stream vanishes, 0.25 mile (400m) ahead. Beyond this is more serious hillwalking. Return to path and follow it back to start.

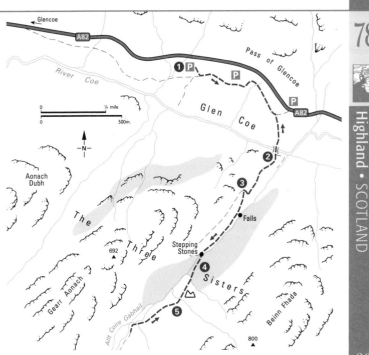

GLEN COE Around The Small Shepherd

Through the mountains.

8 miles/12.9km 4hrs 30min **Ascent** 1,300ft/396m ⚠ **Difficulty** 3
Paths Rough, unmade paths, some boggy bits, no stiles
Map OS Explorer 384 Glen Coe & Glen Etive **Grid ref** NN 213559
Parking Large parking area on south side of A82, marked by yellow AA phone post
WARNING Fords in Lairig Eilde can be impassible or dangerous after heavy rain

1 Signpost to Glen Etive, at edge of car park, marks start of path into Lairig Gartain. Path is clear, but very boggy in places. It heads up-valley with River Coupall down on **L**. Gradually it draws closer to river, but does not cross it. Large cairn marks top of path, which is slightly to **R** of lowest point of pass.

2 Descending path is steeper, first down boggy grass, then stony and eroded to **R** of stream. After 0.5 mile (800m) main path bears off **R**, and slants down **R-H** valley wall. Eventually it emerges on to steep south ridge of Stob Dubh.

3 Path runs to gate in deer fence just below, but do not continue downhill. Follow path above deer fence, descending to cross Allt Lairig Eilde. If stream is too full to cross, return and go down through deer fence to wider, shallower crossing, 200yds (183m) downstream. Alternatively, head up on small path to R of stream, hoping to find safer crossing higher up. After crossing stream, follow fence up to pass its corner. Turn **R** up

wide path that rises out of Glen Etive.

4 Path ascends to **L** of stream, passing waterfalls. Eventually it crosses stream, now very much smaller, then continues straight ahead, crossing col well to **R** of its lowest point. Large cairn marks top of path.

5 New, descending stream is also, confusingly, Allt Lairig Eilde. Path crosses it by wide, shallow ford and goes down its **L** bank. A mile (1.6km) further on, path recrosses, using boulders as stepping stones. It runs to join A82 near cairn that marks entry into Glen Coe.

6 Cross road, and river beyond, to join old Glencoe road at arched culvert. Turn **R** along firm track, which soon rejoins new road, then cross diagonally, on to damp path that runs **R** of new road, then recrosses. It soon rejoins A82 opposite start.

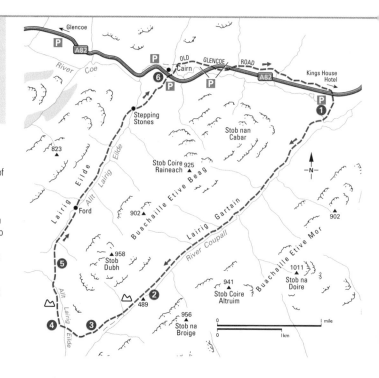

KINLOCHLEVEN Grey Mare's Tail

A ramble down the West Highland Way.

3.5 miles/5.7km 2hrs 15min **Ascent** 984ft/300m ⚠ **Difficulty** ②
Paths Well-made paths, one steep, rough ascent, no stiles
Map OS Explorer 384 Glen Coe & Glen Etive or 392 Ben Nevis & Fort William **Grid ref** NN 187622 on
OS Explorer 384 **Parking** Grey Mare's Tail car park, Kinlochleven

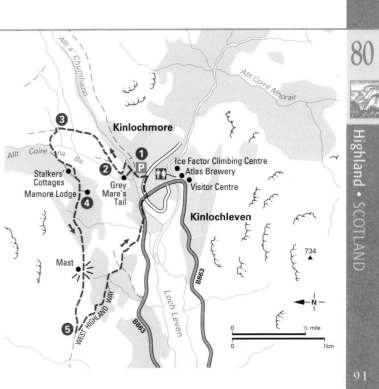

❶ Smooth gravel path leads up out of car park to multicoloured waymarkers pointing **L**. Path rises to view through trees of Grey Mare's Tail waterfall, then descends to footbridge. Here turn **L** (blue waymarker) to visit foot of spectacular waterfall, then return to take path on **R** (white, yellow and green waymarker). Follow stream up for 100yds (91m), then turn **L** at waymarker. Path, quite steep and loose, zig-zags up through birches to reach more open ground.

❷ Path forks. Take **R-H** branch, with yellow and green waymarker, to pass under power lines. Path runs through scattered birch to gate in deer fence, then bends **L** to cross 2 streams. Immediately after 2nd stream is another junction.

❸ Waymarker here has 8 arrows in 4 colours. Turn **L**, following white arrow slightly downhill, to cross footbridge above waterfall and red granite rocks. Path leads up under birches. When path reaches track, turn **L**. Below track is tin deer used for target practice. Signed footpath bypasses Stalkers' Cottages on **L**, then rejoins

track beyond, to junction above Mamore Lodge.

❹ Keep ahead, above lodge, climbing gently past 2 tin huts, self-catering accommodation labelled 'stable' and 'bothy'. At high point of track there is TV mast on **R**, bench on **L** and view along Loch Leven ahead. Track descends gently, with slabs of whitish quartzite above. Wide path of West Highland Way (WHW) can be seen below and gradually rises to join track, with large waymarker planted in cairn.

❺ Turn **L** down West Highland Way path, which drops into woods below. Watch for junction where main path seems to double back to **R**; take smaller path, continuing ahead with WHW waymarker. After crossing tarred access track of Mamore Lodge, path fords small stream to reach village. Turn **L** along pavement and fork **L** into Wades Road to car park.

STRONTIAN The Elements Of Chemistry

To the site of an old lead mine.

7 miles/11.3km 3hrs 45min **Ascent** 950ft/290m **Difficulty** 3

Paths Good through woodland, sketchy on open hill, no stiles

Map OS Explorer 391 Ardgour & Strontian **Grid ref** NM 826633

Parking Nature Reserve car park at Ariundle

1 From car park, continue along track into oak woods. After 0.25 mile (400m), ignore pony path on **R**. In another 0.25 mile (400m) footpath turns off **R**. It crosses Strontian River and heads upstream along it. After pleasant 0.75 mile (1.2km) it recrosses river, following duckboard section to rejoin oakwood track.

2 Turn **R**, away from car park, to reach high gate in deer fence. Track immediately forks. Take downward branch on **R** to emerge into open grazings at river level. Track passes through high gate and ends at gateway and stream.

3 Ford stream on to rough path. This crosses 2 more small streams, then forks (small cairn). The lower, **R-H** branch continues alongside Strontian River, but take **L-H** one, which is quite faint. It slants up to L to solitary holly tree. Here it turns straight uphill for 50yds (46m), then bends **R** to slant up as before, passing 200yds (183m) below bare rock knoll. Remains of wooden steps are in path and few cairns stand beside it. It steepens slightly to pass below small crag with 3

different trees growing out of it – rowan, hazel and oak. With large stream and waterfalls ahead, path turns uphill to brink of small gorge. Above waterfalls, slope eases. Just above, path reaches broken dam wall of former reservoir.

4 Green path runs across slope above. You can turn **R** on this, heading beside stream for about 0.25 mile (400m). Here you will find spoil heap; heather bank marks entrance to adit – mine tunnel running into hill.

5 Return along green path past Point **4**, with remains of Bellsgrove Lead Mines above and below. Path improves into track, following stream down small and slantwise side valley. As this stream turns down to **L**, track contours forward, to cross wooded stream valley by high footbridge above waterfall.

6 Wide, smooth track continues ahead through gate. After 0.5 mile (800m) it rejoins outward route at edge of nature reserve. Follow track back to car park.

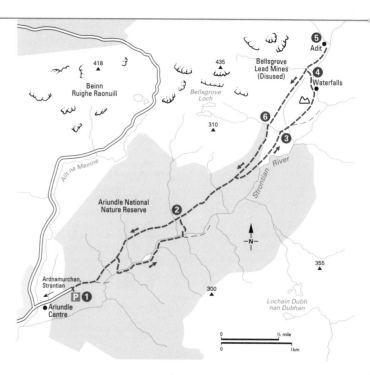

NEVIS GORGE Great Falls

A walk beside Scotland's Himalayan lookalike leading to an enormous waterfall.

2.5 miles/4km 1hr 30min **Ascent** 270ft/82m ⚠ **Difficulty** ⬛1

Paths Well-built path with drops alongside, no stiles
Map OS Explorer 392 Ben Nevis & Fort William **Grid ref** NN 168691
Parking Walkers' car park at end of Glen Nevis road

❶ Note that waterslide above car park is Allt Coire Eoghainn – if you mistake it for Steall Fall and set off towards it you are on a difficult and potentially dangerous path. The path you will take on this walk is much easier, but even here there have been casualties, mostly caused by people wearing unsuitable shoes. At top end of car park a signpost shows no destination closer than 13 miles (21km) to Kinlochleven – accordingly, this walk will be short out-and-back. Well-made path runs gently uphill under woods of birch and hazel, across what turns into very steep slope. For few steps it becomes a rock-cut ledge, with step across waterfall side-stream. Path at this point is on clean pink granite, but you will see boulder of grey schist beside path just afterwards. Ahead, top of Steall Fall can now be just glimpsed through notch of valley.

❷ Path continues downhill to cross stream with big rock blocks; rock now is schist, with fine zig-zag stripes of grey and white. Short rock staircase leads to wooden balcony section. From here path is just above bed of Nevis Gorge. Here river runs through some huge boulders, some of which bridge it completely.

❸ Quite suddenly, path emerges on to level meadow above gorge. Ahead, Steall Fall fills your view. Well-built path runs along **L-H** edge of meadow to point opposite waterfall.

❹ Walk ends here, beside footbridge which consists simply of 3 steel cables over very deep pool. Those who wish to attempt the crossing should note that it gets wobblier in the middle; it's hard to turn round, but the return journey is rather easier. From wire bridge, driest path runs alongside main river round one bend before heading up to foot of waterfall. The view from directly beneath is even more spectacular.

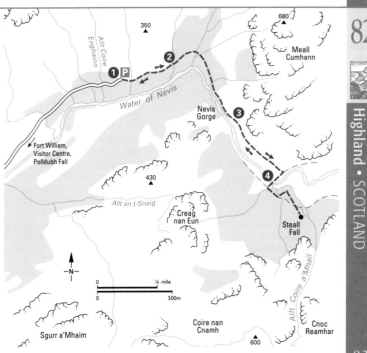

BEN NEVIS Half-Way Up
The great north corrie of Nevis.

10 miles/16.1km 6hrs 15min **Ascent** 2,000ft/610m ⚠ **Difficulty** ③
Paths Hill paths, well-built, then very rough, 4 stiles **Map** OS Explorer 392 Ben Nevis & Fort William
Grid ref NN 123731 **Parking** Large car park at Glen Nevis Visitor Centre

❶ At downstream corner of car park, bridge crosses River Nevis. Path turns upstream, then crosses fields to track. Cross on to signed 'Ben Path' to Ben Nevis. After long climb, notice points you to zig-zag up **L** on to half-way plateau. Path passes above Lochan Meall ant-Suidhe, Halfway Lochan, down on **L**.
❷ Main path takes a sharp turn back to **R**, heading for summit. Path descends ahead, behind wall-like cairn. After 0.25 mile (400m), bear **R** on very rough path that climbs gently over peat bog to cairn on skyline. Here it becomes rough and rocky as it slants down across steep slide slope of valley of Allt a'Mhuilinn. Eventually it joins stream and runs up beside it to Charles Inglis Clark (CIC) Hut.
❸ Return for 100yds (91m) and cross stream on **R** to join clear path downhill. This descends rocky step with waterslide and reaches ladder stile into plantations.
❹ Go down forest road, which bends **L** across bridge, then contours across open hill. After 0.5 mile (800m) main track zig-zags downhill. At slope foot, it passes

under power lines. In another 220yds (200m), take smaller track on **R**, signed 'Distillery', soon to rejoin Allt a'Mhuilinn. Pass between distillery buildings to A82.
❺ Cross River Lochy on Victoria Bridge opposite and turn **L** into fenced-off side road and **L** again along street. It rises to railway bridge. Turn **L** here on long Soldiers Bridge back across Lochy. At its end, turn **R** over stile for riverside path. This soon joins surfaced Great Glen Way path, which becomes built path into woodland. After 2 footbridges, bear **L** on path to edge of Inverlochy. Turn **R**, then **L** into street with copper beeches. This leads through Montrose Square to A82.
❻ Street opposite is signed 'Ben Nevis Footpath'. Shortly, take stone bridge to Glen Nevis road. Turn **L** for 0.25 mile (400m) to track on **L**. Recross Nevis on green footbridge and turn **R** to small riverside footpath. This rejoins road briefly, then leads up-river to footbridge at Glen Nevis Visitor Centre.

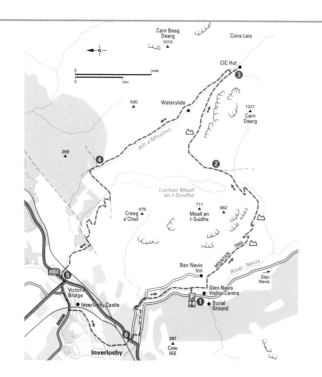

COIRE ARDAIR Happy Birch-Day

Regenerating woodlands lead to a high pass.

8 miles/12.9km 4hrs 15min **Ascent** 1,400ft/427m ⚠ **Difficulty** ③
Paths Very good, rough around the loch, no stiles
Map OS Explorer 401 Loch Laggan & Creag Meagaidh **Grid ref** NN 483872
Parking Nature reserve car park at Aberarder track end beside Loch Laggan

❶ New path runs alongside grey gravel track, leading to Aberarder farm. Here there's information area and bench under roof. Pass **R** of buildings following footprint waymarker on to rebuilt path.

❷ Well-built path rises through bracken, then crosses boggy area. It heads up valley of Allt Coire Ardair, keeping little way up **R-H** side, becoming steeper as it ascends through area of regenerating birch trees. Now crags of Coire Ardair come into sight ahead. Path crosses many small streams – here it is still being reconstructed. It bends **L**, slightly downhill, to join main river. Path winds gently near stream, then suddenly to outflow of Lochan a'Choire.

❸ Outflow is fine viewpoint for crag walls of Coire Ardair. These walls are too loose and overgrown for rock climbing, but when covered in snow and hoarfrost give excellent sport for winter mountaineers. Circuit of lochan is considerably more rugged than path up glen, and could be omitted if outflow stream is too full, or if picnic is preferred. Cross outflow stream near where it emerges from lochan and follow trace of path round shore to notable clump of boulders marked by stretcher box. (The stretcher is used for removing mountain casualties from the foot of the crags.) One boulder forms small cave, with spring running through it. A vigorous rowan tree, seeded where deer can't get at it, shows that without grazing pressure this glen would be wooded even at this altitude of 2,000ft (610m).

❹ After boulder cave you must cross rocks and scree. This short section is awkward. Once past head of lochan, slant up away from shore. Path descends from high on **L**, coming out of notch called Window. Join this and turn down to loch's outflow (Point ❸ again). Quite clearly there's no way out of this dead-end valley that doesn't involve serious mountain walking – or one of those winter climbs up icy gullies. Return down valley by outward path.

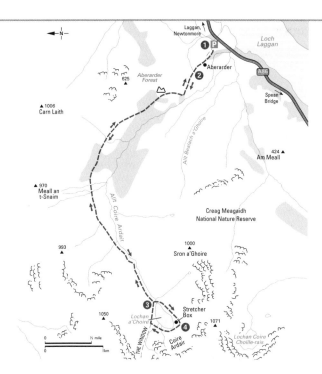

FORT AUGUSTUS Up And Down The Corrieyairack
On the road the English built.

7.25 miles/11.7km 4hrs **Ascent** 1,300ft/395m **Difficulty** [3]
Paths Tracks, one vanished pathless section, 2 stiles **Map** OS Explorer 400 Loch Lochy & Glen Roy
Grid ref NH 378080 **Parking** South edge of Fort Augustus, signed lane from A82 to burial ground

❶ Track leads round to **L** of burial ground to meet minor road. Turn **R** for about 0.25 mile (400m) to foot of rather rubbly track signposted for Corrieyairack Pass. After some 50yds (46m) track passes through gate, getting much easier, and, soon, the right of way joins smoother track coming up from Culachy House.

❷ After another 0.25 mile (400m), gate leads out on to open hill. About 350yds (320m) further on, track passes under high-tension wires. At once bear **L** across meadow. As this drops towards stream, green track slants down **R**. Bear **L** off track to pass corner of deer fence, where small path continues to stream. Cross and turn downstream on old grassy track. It recrosses stream and passes under high power line to bend.

❸ Turn **R** across high stone bridge. Disused track climbs through birch woods then, as terraced shelf, across high side of Glen Tarff. Side stream forms wooded re-entrant ahead. Old track contours in to this and crosses below narrow waterfall – former bridge has now disappeared.

❹ Contour out across steep slope to pick up old track as it restarts. It runs gently uphill to gateless gateway in fence. Turn up fence to another gateway above. Here turn **L** for 20yds (18m) to brink of another stream hollow. (Its Gaelic name – Sidhean Ceum na Goibhre – means 'Fairy Goat-step'.) Don't go into this, but turn uphill alongside it, through pathless bracken, to its top. Deer fence is above; turn **L** alongside it to go through nearby gate, then **L** beside fence. When it turns downhill, green path continues ahead, gently uphill through heather. Ahead and above, pylons crossing skyline mark Corrieyairack Pass. Path bends **R** to join Corrieyairack track just above.

❺ Turn **R**. Track passes knoll on **R**, highest point of this walk. It then descends in curves for 1.25 miles (2km). Pass is still technically road, and it is now scheduled ancient monument, protected by law. From here track climbs gently to rejoin upward route. At final bend, stile offers short cut through ancient burial ground.

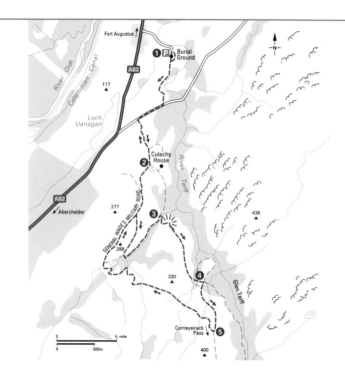

LOCH AN EILEIN Castle On The Island

The castle on the island in the loch is the heart of the Rothiemurchus Forest.

4.25 miles/6.8km 1hr 45min **Ascent** 100ft/30m ⚠ **Difficulty** ☐1

Paths Wide smooth paths, optional steep hill with high ladder stile
Map OS Explorer 403 Cairn Gorm & Aviemore **Grid ref** NH 897084
Parking Estate car park near Loch an Eilein, charges apply

❶ From end of car park, made-up path leads to visitor centre. Turn **L** to cross end of Loch an Eilein, then turn **R** on sandy track. Loch shore is on **R**. Small paths lead down to it if you wish to visit. Just past red-roofed house, deer fence runs across, with gate.
❷ Track becomes wide, smooth path close to loch. After bridge, main track forks **R** to pass bench backed by flat boulder. Smaller path on **L** leads into hills and through pass of Lairig Ghru, eventually to Braemar. After crossing stream at low concrete footbridge, path bends **R** for 120yds (110m) to junction. Just beyond you'll find footbridge with wooden handrails.
❸ To shorten walk, cross this footbridge and continue along main track, passing Point ❹ in another 170yds (155m). For longer walk, turn **L** before footbridge on to narrower path that will pass around Loch Gamhna. This 2nd loch soon appears on your **R**. Where path forks, keep **R** to pass along loch side, across its head (rather boggy) and back along its further side, to rejoin wider path around Loch an Eilein. Turn **L** here.

❹ Continue around Loch an Eilein, with water on your **R**, to reedy corner of loch and bench. About 55yds (51m) further, path turns sharply **R**, signposted 'footpath'. After gate, turn **R** to loch side and a memorial to Major General Brook Rice who drowned here while skating. Follow shore to point opposite castle, then back up to wide track above. Deer fence on **L** leads back to visitor centre.
❺ From here, stiff climb (500ft/152m) can be made on to rocky little hill of Ord Ban. Cross ladder stile immediately to **R** of toilet block and follow deer fence to **R** for 150yds (137m), to point behind car park. Just behind one of lowest birches on slope, small indistinct path zig-zags up steep slope. It slants to **L** to avoid crags, then crosses small rock slab (take care if wet) and continues on to summit. Descend by same path.

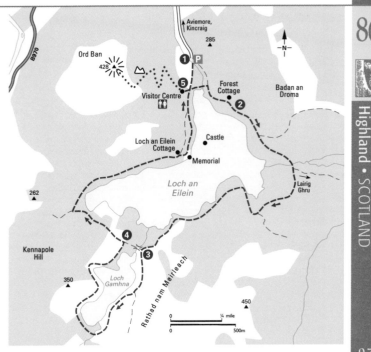

GLENMORE The Thieves' Road

To the lochan, once the haunt of fairy folk.

5 miles/8km 2hrs 15min **Ascent** 400ft/122m ⚠ **Difficulty** 2

Paths Smooth tracks, one steep ascent, no stile
Map OS Explorer 403 Cairn Gorm & Aviemor **Grid ref** NH 980095
Parking Bridge just south of Glenmore village

① Head upstream on sandy track to **L** of river. Interpretation signs explain the flowers of the forest you may come across, many are ferns and mosses. After 550yds (503m), turn **L** on wide smooth path with blue/yellow waymarkers. Ahead is gate into Glenmore Lodge rifle range; here path bends **R**, to wide gravel track.

② Turn **R**, away from Glenmore Lodge, to cross concrete bridge into Caledonian Reserve. Immediately keep ahead on smaller track (blue waymarker) as main one bends **R**. Track narrows as it heads into Pass of Ryvoan between steep wooded slopes of pine, birch and scree. At this most scenic part of route, path turns **L**, with blue waymarker, which you take in a moment. Just beyond, steps on **R** lead down to Lochan Uaine. Walk round to **L** of water on beach. At head of loch small path leads back up to track. Turn sharp **L**, back to junction already visited; now turn off to R on to narrower path with blue waymarker.

③ This small path crosses duckboard and heads back down valley. Very soon it starts to climb steeply to **R**, up rough stone steps. When it levels, going is easier, although it's still narrow with tree roots. Path reaches forest road at bench and waymarker.

④ Continue to **L** along track. After clear-felled area with views, track re-enters trees and slopes downhill into Glenmore village. Just above main road turn **R**, through green barrier, to reach Glenmore Visitor Centre. Pass through its car park to main road.

⑤ Cross to Glenmore shop. Behind post-box, steps lead down to campsite. Pass along its **R-H** edge to path into woods. Head **L** across footbridge to shore of Loch Morlich and follow beaches until another river blocks way. Turn **L** along river bank. Ignore footbridge, but continue on wide path with river on **R**. Where path divides, smaller branch continues beside river through bushes to car park.

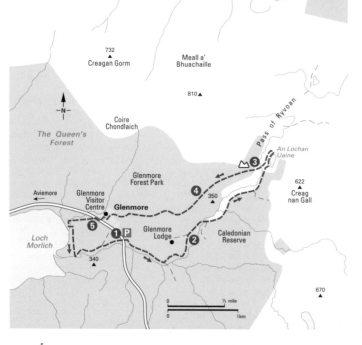

GLENELG Over The Sea To Skye

Along the coast with views to Skye.

8.5 miles/13.7km 4hrs **Ascent** 1,000ft/300m ⚠ **Difficulty** ☐1

Paths Tracks, grassy shoreline, minor road, 4 stiles
Map OS Explorer 413 Knoydart, Loch Hourn & Loch Duich **Grid ref** NG 795213
Parking Above pier of Glenelg ferry

1 Track runs out of car park, signed 'Ardintoul and Totaig'. It descends through 2 gates, then goes up through 3rd into plantation. With power lines above, track forks. Take **L-H** one, downhill, passing arrow made of stones. Track runs between feet of pylon and climbs again to contour through wood. It runs in and out of stream gorge, then descends towards shore. On other side of Loch Alsh, Balmacara is ahead.

2 At shoreline, track disappears into open field strip. Follow short grass next to shingle beach, passing salmon farm just offshore. When trees once more run down to sea, green track runs next to shore to reach open field below small crag with birches. Keep along shore, outside field walls, and sometimes taking to stripy schist shingle, towards square brick building on point ahead. As you pass end of birch crag, you come to wall gap. Here track that's simply pair of green ruts runs directly inland through grey gate to meet gravel track. Turn **L**, away from abandoned Ardintoul farm to pass sheds and house to regain shoreline at Ardintoul.

3 Track runs along shoreline, then turns inland to climb hill behind. Steeper uphill sections are tarred. Below on **L**, Allt na Dalach runs into Loch Alsh, with example of a gravel spit where river debris runs into tidal water. Track enters plantations, crosses stream and bends **R** to complete climb to Bealach Luachrach.

4 Divert here to Glas Bheinn – tough little hill, but fine viewpoint. (Grading and timing don't take account of side-trip.) From road's high point, turn **R** up wet tree gap to open hillside. Follow remains of old fence up 1st rise. Where it bends **R**, continue ahead up to summit, returning by same route. Old fence makes useful guide back into tree gap. Continue downhill from Point **4** on unsurfaced road, which reaches tarred road 1 mile (1.6km) north of Glenelg village. Grassy shoreline, then road, leads back to ferry pier.

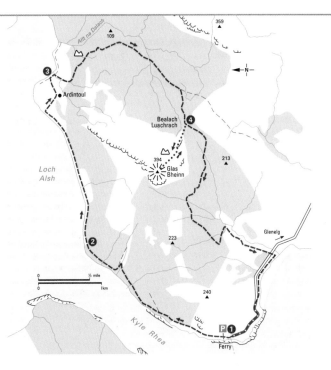

GLENBRITTLE Heart Of The Cuillins
Classic rock-climbing country.

5.75 miles/9.2km 4hrs **Ascent** 1,900ft/580m ⚠ **Difficulty** ③
Paths Mountain paths, one boggy and tough, 2 stiles **Map** OS Explorer 411 Skye – Cuillin Hills
Grid ref NG 409206 **Parking** Walkers' pull-off before gate into Glenbrittle campsite

❶ From parking area, track leads on through Glenbrittle campsite to gate with kissing gate. Pass **L** of toilet block to cross stile. Turn **L** along stony track just above, which runs gently downhill above campsite, to rejoin Glenbrittle road.

❷ Keep ahead to cross bridge with white Memorial Hut just ahead. On **R** are stone buchts (sheep-handling enclosures) and here waymarked path heads uphill to reach footbridge which crosses Allt Coire na Banachdich.

❸ Cross footbridge and head up to **R** of stream's deep ravine, with great view of waterfall at its head. Its Gaelic name, Eas Mor, means simply 'Big Waterfall'. Above, path bears **R**, to slant up hillside. Below spur of Sgurr Dearg path forks. Here keep **R**, aiming for **R-H** of 2 corries above, which is Coire Lagan. Path passes above Loch an Fhir-bhallaich. After short steepening, rebuilding works currently end and path becomes rough. It rounds shoulder into lower part of Coire Lagan and meets much larger path at big cairn.

❹ Turn uphill on this path, until belt of bare rock blocks way into upper corrie. This rock has been smoothed by glacier into gently rounded swells, known as 'boiler-plates'. Scree field runs up into boiler-plate rocks. Best way keeps up **L** edge, below slab wall with small waterslide, to highest point of scree. Head up **L** for 50ft (15m) on bare rock, then back **R** on ledges to eroded scree above boiler-plate obstruction. Look back down your upward route to note it for your return. Trodden way slants up to **R**. With main stream near by on **R**, it goes up to rim of upper corrie.

❺ Boiler-plate slabs at lochan's outflow are excellent for picnics. Walking mainly on bare rock, it's easy to make circuit of lochan. For return journey, retrace your steps to Point ❹. Ignoring **R** fork of route you came up by, keep straight downhill on main path. It runs straight down to toilets at Glenbrittle campsite. Turn **L** over a rustic footbridge to finish along beach.

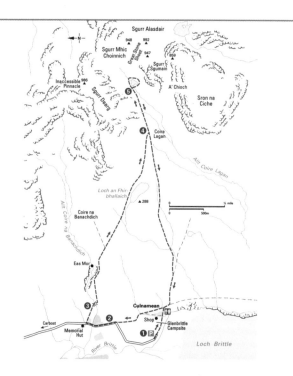

QUIRAING Prison And Pinnacle

Skye's northern peninsula lava landscape.

5.25 miles/8.4km 3hrs **Ascent** 1,200ft/365m ⚠ **Difficulty** ☒

Paths Well-used path, 2 stiles **Map** OS Explorer 408 Skye – Trotternish & the Storr

Grid ref NG 440679 **Parking** Pull-in, top of pass on Staffin–Uig road. Overflow parking at cemetery 0.25 mile (400m) on Staffin side (not available during funerals)

❶ Well-built path starts at green signpost opposite lay-by, where you can park. Jagged tower of grass and rock on skyline is The Prison. Path crosses steep landslip slope towards it, with awkward crossing of small stream gully on bare rock, then passes waterfall high above and heads to **R**, rather than up into rocky gap. It turns uphill into wide col **L** of The Prison.

❷ Main path goes forward, slightly uphill, crossing new fence at stile and then dodging below crag foot. It crosses foot of steep ground, then passes above small peat pool. Ignore path forking down **R**; main path slants up to **L** into col where old wall runs across.

❸ Path descends into landslip valley that runs across rather than down hillside, then slants **L** to col with stile.

❹ Cross and turn **R** for excursion to Sron Vourlinn. Follow crest over slightly rocky section with short descent beyond, then join main path along grassy meadow with very sudden edge on **R**. After highest point, continue slightly downhill to north top. Here you can see that land is still slipping, with crevasse beside

cliff edge where another narrow section is shortly to peel away. Shelter of rock crevice grows luxuriant rock rose, rowan and valerian.

❺ Return to col with stile (Point ❹) and continue uphill. Drops are now on **L**, as you look down towards pinnacles surrounding The Table. After passing broken ground on **R**, you come to fallen wall, part of which appears from below as cairn. Path continues next to cliff edge on **L**; you can fork **R**, directly uphill, to summit trig point on Meall na Suiramach.

❻ Follow broad faint path slightly downhill to cairn at cliff edge. You now look straight down on to The Table, 100ft (30m) below. Turn **R** on wide path alongside crag drop. After 0.25 mile (400m) as path steepens, you'll see fence on **R** with kissing gate. Once through this, path becomes much clearer, contouring across steep slope of Maoladh Mor. Above car park, it turns straight downhill for final ascent.

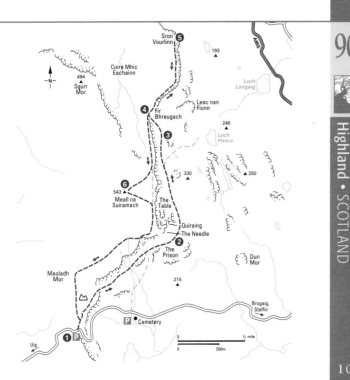

RAASAY A Royal Refuge
To Raasay's old iron mining railway.

7.75 miles/12.5km 3hrs 45min **Ascent** 820ft/250m ⚠ **Difficulty** 2

Paths Small but clear paths, some tracks, 1 stile **Map** OS Explorer 409 Raasay, Rona & Scalpay or 410 Skye – Portree & Bracadale **Grid ref** NG 555342 **Parking** Ferry terminal at Sconser (or lay-by to east)

❶ Turn **L** on island's small road. At Inverarish, turn **L** over bridge and divert **L** past cottages and along shore. After playing field you rejoin road, which leads past Isle of Raasay Hotel to another road junction.

❷ Uamh na Ramh souterrain is over stile on **L**. Continue past stable block (ahead is Raasay House, an outdoor centre). At corner of stable, turn **L**, signed 'Clachan'. Track continues below ramparts of old gun battery. From pier, follow path around bay, until gate leads to shoreline path to Eilean Aird nan Gobhar. Check tides before crossing rocks to this tidal island.

❸ Head inland over rock knoll, then pass along the **L-H** edge of plantation on muddy path overhung by rhododendron. Continue along shore of North Bay, with pine plantation on **R**, round to headland. Go up briefly through low basalt cliff and return along its top. Head along **L** edge of plantation, to emerge through decorative iron gate on to road.

❹ Turn **L** for 180yds (165m) to grey gate on **R**. Green track leads up and to **R** into craggy valley. At walled paddock it turns **L** and to **R** to join tarred track. Follow

this past lily lochan (Loch a' Mhuilinn) and turn **L** across its dam. Join wide path running up under larch and rhododendron but, in 100yds (91m), bear **R**, waymarked 'Temptation Hill Trail'. Look for side path on **R** which leads up to Dun Bhorogh Dail (Iron Age tower). Main path leads down to pass austere white church, then bends to **R** and drops to tarred road.

❺ Turn sharp **L** up road for 0.25 mile (400m), then **R** at signpost for Burma Road. Track shrinks to path as it bends **L** and climbs steeply. It becomes forest track, passing white waymarkers, reaching abandoned buildings of old iron mine.

❻ When you get to tarred road beyond, turn up **L** to signpost for Miners' Trail. Here turn **R** on green track of former railway. Where viaduct has been removed, new-built path descends steeply and then climbs again to regain railbed. Blue-waymarked Miners' Trail turns off, but route follows railway onwards, across stretch of moor and down to ferry terminal.

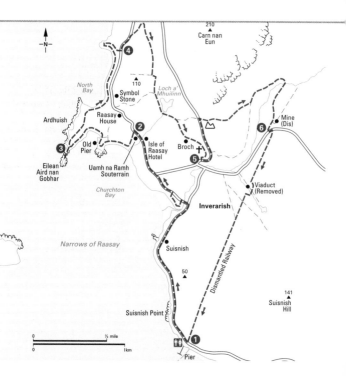

PORTREE Seeing Sea Eagles

A lovely coastal walk to a raised beach called the Bile.

3.5 miles/5.5km 1hr 15min **Ascent** 459ft/140m ⚠ **Difficulty** ☐1☐
Paths Smooth, well-made paths, farm track, 3 stiles
Map OS Explorer 409 Raasay, Rona & Scalpay or 410 Skye – Portree & Bracadale
Parking On A855 (Staffin Road) above Portree Bay. Another small parking area near slipway

❶ Turn off A855 on to lane signed 'Budh Mor', walk to shoreline and then continue to small parking area. Tarred path continues along shore past slipway. After footbridge, it passes under hazels. Path passes below viewpoint with flagpoles and then rounds headland to reach edge of level green field called The Bile.
❷ Wall runs up edge of The Bile. Sign points up **L** for Scorybreck but ignore it and go through small gate ahead. Rough path leads into corner of The Bile field. Go up its **L** edge and turn across its top, to stile just above field gate. Cross top of next field on old green path, to stile at its corner. See track just beyond.
❸ Turn sharp **L**, up track. At top it passes through 2 gates to reach stony road just **R** of Torvaig. Turn **L** past house and cross foot of tarred road into gently descending track. It runs down between 2 large corrugated sheds and then through gate with stile.
❹ Grassy path ahead leads down into Portree, but you can take a short, rather rough, diversion to Dun Torvaig (ancient fortified hilltop) above. For dun, turn

L along fence, and **L** again on well-made path above. It leads to kissing gate above 2 sheds. Turn sharp **R** along fence for few steps, then bear **L** around base of small outcrop and head straight up on tiny path to dun. Remnants of dry-stone walling can be seen around summit. Return to well-made path, passing above Point ❹ to join wall on **R**. Path leads down under goat willows into wood where it splits; stay close to wall.
❺ At 1st houses (The Parks Bungalow 5), keep downhill on tarred street. On **L** is entrance to Cuillin Hills Hotel. A few steps later, fork **R** on to stony path. At shore road, turn **R** across stream and at once **R** again on path that runs up for 60yds (55m) to craggy little waterfall. Return to shore road and turn **R** to start.

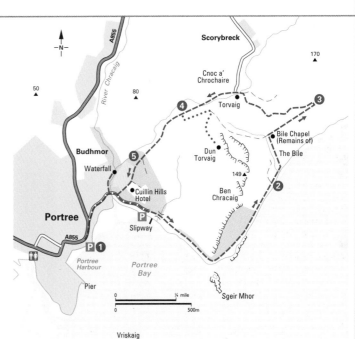

RAMASAIG Waterstein Head

Through crofting country and peat moors to a 1,000ft (305m) sea cliff.

5.75 miles/9.2km 3hrs 30min **Ascent** 1,500ft/457m ⚠ **Difficulty** 2

Paths Grassy clifftops and moorland, 2 fences and 1 gate

Map OS Explorer 407 Skye – Dunvegan **Grid ref** NG 163443

Parking Ramasaig road end or pull-ins at pass 0.75 mile (1.2km) north

① From end of tarmac, road continues as track past farm buildings, with bridge over Ramasaig Burn. After gate it reaches shed with tin roof. Bear R and follow **L** bank of Ramasaig Burn to shore.

② Cross burn at ford and head up very steep meadow beside fence that protects cliff edge. There's awkward fence to cross half-way up. At top, above Ramasaig Cliff, keep following fence on **L**. It cuts across to **R** to protect notch in cliff edge. From here, you could cut down to parking areas at nearby road pass.

③ Keep downhill along cliffside fence. At bottom, turf wall off to **R** provides another short-cut back to road. Clifftop walk now bears slightly **R** around V-notch of Moonen Burn. Small path crosses stream and slants up **L** to rejoin clifftop fence, which soon turns slightly inland around another cliff notch. Cliff-edge fence leads up and to **L**, to reach Waterstein Head. Here is trig point, 971ft (296m) above sea – 2nd highest cliff on Skye. Below, see Neist Point lighthouse.

④ Return for 0.25 mile (400m) down to where fence bends **R**, then continue through shallow grassy col for slight rise to Beinn Charnach. Here bear **R** to follow gently rounded grass ridge-line parallel with cliffs. Highest line along ridge is driest. Fence runs across, with grey gate at its highest point where it passes through col. Climb over gate and on up to cairn on Beinn na Coinnich.

⑤ Continue along slightly rocky plateau for 300yds (274m) to southeast top. Now Ramasaig road is visible 0.25 mile (400m) away on L. Go down to join quad-bike track heading towards road. Just before reaching road, bike track crosses swampy col. This shows old and recent peat workings. Turn **R**, along road, passing above Loch Eishort to start.

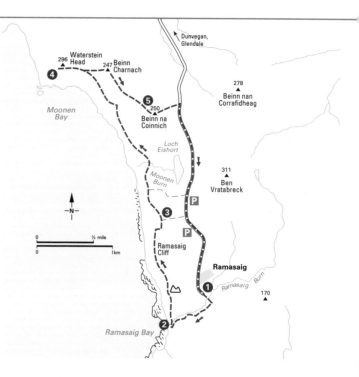

STRATH CARRON South Torridon Mountains

Deer Stalkers' paths lead into the mountains.

9 miles/14.5km 5hrs **Ascent** 1,700ft/518m **⚠ Difficulty** ☒
Paths Well-made path, then track, no stiles
Map OS Explorer 429 Glen Carron & West Monar **Grid ref** NH 005484
Parking On A890 below Achnashellach Station **NOTE** During stalking season on Achnashellach Estate (15 September–20 October, not Sundays), keep strictly to route, which is right of way

❶ Track to station runs up behind phone box, then turns **R** to reach platform end. Cross line through 2 gates and head up stony track opposite, past waymarker arrow. After 100yds (91m) reach junction under power lines. Turn **L** on smooth gravel road to gate through deer fence. After 0.25 mile (400m), look for signpost where new path turns back to **L**.
❷ Path returns through deer fence at pothole type, then runs up alongside River Lair. As slope steepens above tree-line, short side path on **L** gives waterfall view. Stalkers' path runs over slabs of bare sandstone. Cairn marks point where it arrives in upper valley, Coire Lair, with view to high pass at its head, 2 miles (3.2km) away.
❸ About 200yds (183m) after 1st cairn, another marks paths junction. Bear **R**, between 2 pools. Next junction has well-built cairn. Bear **R**, on path that leaves corrie through wide, shallow col just 350yds (320m) above. Elegant conical cairn marks final path junction. Bear **R**; in few steps head downhill above path. Path runs downhill

among drumlins and sandstone boulders, slanting down to **R** to join Allt nan Dearcag. Path now runs down alongside this stream. Path drops to reach footbridge. This bridge crosses side stream, Allt Coire Beinne Leithe, with Easan Geal, White Waterfalls, just above.
❹ At open bothy shelter hut, track continues downhill, with gorge of Easan Dorcha on its **R**. After 1 mile (1.6km) reach stone bridge on **R**. Cross, on to track that runs up wide, open valley to Coulin Pass at its head.
❺ After pass, track goes through gate into plantations, then bends **R** to slant down side of Strath Carron. At Scottish Rights of Way Society signpost, follow main track ahead towards Achnashellach. Coss bridge to mobile phone mast. Fork **L**, just before 2nd mast, and descend to reach junction above Achnashellach Station.

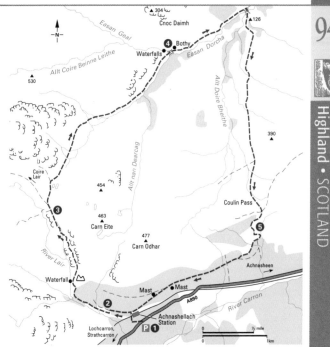

LOCH TORRIDON The Diabaig Coast Path

In the footsteps of the fairy folk.

9.5 miles/15.3km 6hrs **Ascent** 1,805ft/550m ▲ **Difficulty** 3

Paths Narrow, rough and wet in places, no stiles **Map** OS Explorer 433 Torridon – Beinn Eighe & Liathach **Grid ref** NG 842073 **Parking** Wester Alligin, pull-off on side road near Alligin River

❶ From parking place, follow road over Abhainn Alligin river. Path leads along shoreline for 100yds (91m) and continues up **R** among sandstone outcrops. Bear **L** under power line to join corner of tarmac driveway. Keep ahead to reach Wester Alligin.

❷ Turn up road and then **L**, on road for Diabaig. As road steepens, you can take path **R** of power lines, rejoining track across high pass and then down past 2 lochs – Loch Diabaigas Airde and Loch a'Mhullaich.

❸ Turn off **L**, crossing outflow of Loch a'Mhullaich on footbridge. Clear path leads out along high wall of stream valley, then zig-zags down to grey gate. Go down through woods to white house, No 1 Diabaig. Turn **R** to reach old stone pier.

❹ Return up path you just came down to pass stone shed. Sign indicates **R** turn, under an outcrop and between boulders. Path heads up to small rock step with arrow mark and tree root you can hold on to. It then leads up to gate in fence and zig-zags into open gully with large crag on **R**. At top, it turns **R** along shelf, with more crag above. Path slants down along foot of

another crag, then up to col, with last view of Diabaig.

❺ Path bends **R** to Loch a' Bhealaich Mhoir and then turns **L** below it to Lochan Dubh. Cross outbound slant **L** towards cottage of Port Laire.

❻ Pass above house, then slant gradually away from sea. Path crosses head of bracken valley with ruined croft house into bleak knolly area. Cross 2 branches of stream and go up to cairn which marks where path bears **L** up spur. It now contours across heathery meadow among knolls. At end it climbs pink rocks over final spur. Just ahead is gate in deer fence.

❼ Path leads along level shelf with views to Liathach and head of Loch Torridon, then it crosses high, steep slope of heather. Near end of slope, path forks. Take upper branch, to go through wide col. Boggy path heads down towards Wester Alligin. From gate above village, faint path runs down in direction of green shed. It descends through wood, then contours above village to road above Point ❷. Retrace steps to start.

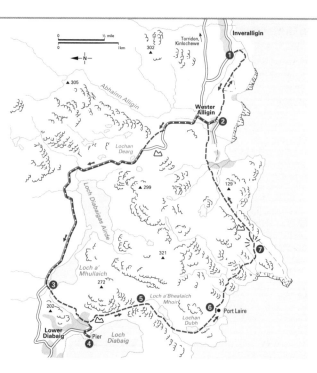

GAIRLOCH Flowerdale Falls

Porpoise-watching along the Gairloch shore.

5.25 miles/8.4km 2hrs 45min **Ascent** 800ft/244m ⚠ **Difficulty** ☐1

Paths Tracks and smooth paths, mostly waymarked, no stiles

Map OS Explorer 433 Torridon – Beinn Eighe & Liathach or 434 Gairloch & Loch Ewet

Grid ref NG 807756 (OS Explorer 433) **Parking** Beach car park, southern end of Gairloch

❶ Cross road and head up to **R** of newer cemetery. Turn **L** at its corner, going into trees to path above. Turn **R** until footbridge leads on to wide path that soon runs downhill. Main path bends **R** (green-top waymarker) and runs down to tarred driveway.

❷ Turn **L** along tarred track to pass Flowerdale House. Track passes **L** of barn and turns **R** at waterfall sign to pass Gairloch Trekking Centre. In about 0.25 mile (400m) you pass timber-surfaced bridge on **R**.

❸ Follow main path ahead, still to **L** of stream to reach footbridge built by Royal Engineers, just before you get to Flowerdale Waterfall.

❹ Path leads past waterfall to cross footbridge above. It runs up into pine clump, then turns down valley. After another footbridge it joins rough track. Pass memorial to blind piper of Gairloch, just before forest road beside Point ❸. Turn **L**, away from timber-surfaced bridge, through felled forest that's regenerating naturally.

❺ Blue-topped pole marks path to **R** with footbridge. It leads through scrub birch and bracken with blue waymarker poles. Path bends **R** at old fence cornerpost and down to pass above and to **L** of enclosed field. Turn **R** underneath 2 large oak trees and cross small stream to earth track.

❻ Turn **L** for few steps, until bracken path runs up **R** past waymarked power pole. Path bends **L** under oaks, then drops to rejoin earth track. This soon meets larger track (old road from Loch Maree to Gairloch). Turn **R** on this, through 2 gates, to Old Inn at Charlestown.

❼ Cross old bridge, and main road, towards pier. Turn **R** at signpost for beach, to stepped path to **L** of Gairloch Chandlery. Tarred path passes **L** of pine wood, then turns **R** into trees. It bends **L** and emerges to run along spine of small headland. Just before being carried out to sea it turns sharp **R**, and crosses above rocky bay to fort (An Dun). Duckboard path runs along back of beach, then turns **R** to car park.

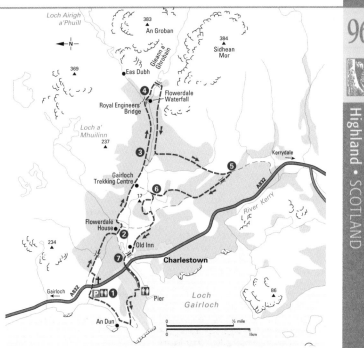

POOLEWE Great Wilderness

A pleasant walk around Loch Kernsary.

6.5 miles/10.4km 2hrs 45min **Ascent** 250ft/76m ⚠ **Difficulty** 2
Paths Mostly good, but one short rough, wet section, 3 stiles **Map** OS Explorer 434 Gairloch & Loch Ewe
Grid ref NG 857808 **Parking** In Poolewe, just up B8057 side street

① Kissing gate beside public toilets leads to path that crosses Marie Curie Field of Hope to main road. Turn **L** to cross bridge over River Ewe and then through village. At 40mph derestriction sign, there's white cottage on **R**. Beside it, tarred trackway has Scottish Rights of Way Society signpost for Kernsary.
② Follow track over cattle grid to new track that forks **L**. After 50yds (46m), keep ahead on path with wall on **L**. It passes through kissing gate into Cnoc na Lise, Garden Hill. This has been replanted as a community wood with oak and birch trees. Another kissing gate leads out of the young wood. Good, reconstructed path runs through gorse and then under low-voltage power line. It crosses low spur to fine view of Loch Kernsary and remote, steep-sided hills of Great Wilderness, then crosses stream to loch side.
③ Path follows **L-H** shore of loch, passing through patches of birch scrub. After stile, near loch head, it suddenly deteriorates, becoming braided trod of boulder and bog. Past loch head, slant to **L** down

meadow to find footbridge under oak tree. Head up, with fence on **R**, to join track beside Kernsary farm.
④ Turn **R**, through gate. Follow track past farm, to culvert crossing of Kernsary River. This becomes ford only after heavy rain. If needed, find footbridge 70yds (64m) upstream. After crossing, turn **R** on smooth track. New track bears **L**, away from Loch Kernsary towards hollow containing Loch Maree. After bridge over Inveran River is gate with ladder stile. Signs welcoming responsible walkers (and cyclists) reflect principles of Letterewe Accord. Soon come 1st views of Loch Maree. Driveway of Inveran house joins from **L** and track starts being tarred.
⑤ At 'Blind Corners' sign green track on **L** leads down to point where narrow loch imperceptibly becomes wide river. Return to main track and follow it above and then beside River Ewe. It reaches Poolewe just beside bridge.

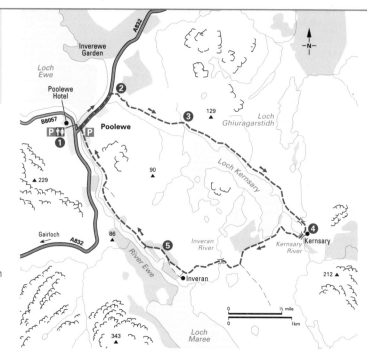

LOCH NESS Monsters And Beasties

Overlooking Loch Ness and past the home of the Beast of Boleskine.

4.25 miles/6.8km 2hrs 15min **Ascent** 700ft/213m ⚠ **Difficulty** 2

Paths Waymarked paths and tracks, no stiles **Map** OS Explorer 416 Inverness, Loch Ness & Culloden

Grid ref NH 522237 **Parking** Forest Enterprise car park

1 Follow yellow waymarkers uphill near stream. After 100yds (91m), path on **R** has yellow-top waymarker. After bench, path contours briefly then turns up **L**, to higher viewpoint. It then turns back sharply **R** and descends on earth steps through little crag to forest road. Turn **R** for 200yds (183m).

2 Turn up **L** on footpath with more yellow waymarkers. Path has low, heavily mossed wall alongside as it bends up to forest road. Turn **R** and walk for about 150yds (137m) to sharp **L-H** bend. Turn off **R** here, on small footpath through small trees, then go steeply up **L** under mature trees. At top, bear **L** along ridge, dropping gently to fine viewpoint.

3 Return for 100yds (91m) and bear **L** down other side of ridge. Path now drops steeply to forest road. Sign indicates Lochan Torr an Tuill, on **L**.

4 Return along forest road, past where you joined it. It climbs gently and then descends to sharp **R** bend where you turned off earlier – waymarker says 'to Carpark' on side facing you. After 150yds (137m), at

another 'to Car Park' waymarker, turn **L** down path with low mossed wall to forest road (Point **2**). Turn **L**, past red/green waymarker. Track kinks **L** past quarry.

5 Where main track bends **R**, downhill, keep ahead on green track with red/green waymarker. It emerges from trees at signpost. Follow this down **R** towards Easter Boleskine house. Green waymarkers indicate diversion to **L** of house, to join its driveway track below. Follow this down to B852.

6 Turn **R** for 50yds (46m). Below **L** edge of road is tarred track. Turn down faint path between trees to cross this track, with blue waymarker leading into clearer path beyond. Pass down **R** of electricity transformers. At slope foot, main path bears **R** with blue waymarker. It runs above loch shore and joins gravel track below Lower Birchwood House. At turning circle, jetty on **L** is great for monster-watchers. Tarred lane ahead leads to B852, with car park above on **R**.

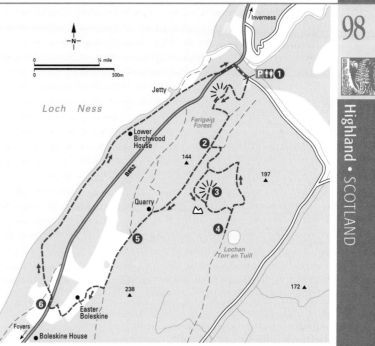

STRATHPEFFER The Falls Of Rogie
From a spa to a salmon-leaping waterfall.

10 miles/16.1km 5hrs **Ascent** 1,200ft/365m **⚠ Difficulty** ☐1
Paths Waymarked paths and track, no stiles **Map** OS Explorer 437 Ben Wyvis & Strathpeffer
Grid ref NH 483582 **Parking** Main square, Strathpeffer

❶ Head along main road towards Contin. At edge of town, turn **R** at metal signpost for Garve then, at bend in lane, turn **L**, following another signpost.
❷ Follow track to **L** of Loch Kinellan. As it bends **R**, keep ahead up path beside tall bushes to corner of plantation. Here join larger track leading into forest. Continue for 0.5 mile (800m) until it reaches signpost.
❸ Turn **L** for View Rock on good path with green waymarkers. After long descent, ignore green path turning off **L** and follow green waymarkers downhill. At forest road go straight over beside signpost. Path crosses 2two more forest roads to Contin Forest car park.
❹ At end of car park pick up wide path signed 'River Walk'. Where red waymarkers turn back **R**, keep ahead on path with deer head markers. It bends up **R** beside stream to forest road. Turn **L**, signposted 'Garve', and in another 80yds (73m) bear **L**, heading downhill.
❺ Go on for 600yds (549m), when small track on **L** is signed 'Rogie Falls Bridge'. At its foot, cross spectacular footbridge below falls and turn **R**,

upstream. Path has green waymarkers and after 0.25 mile (400m) bends **L** away from river. It crosses rocky ground to junction. Turn up **R**, to Rogie Falls car park.
❻ Leave car park through wooden arch and follow green waymarkers back to bridge. Retrace route to Point **❺** and turn sharp **L** up another forest road, leading uphill to where much fainter track crosses.
❼ Turn **R** down smaller track to pass between obstructing boulders, to signpost. Turn **L**, signed 'Strathpeffer'. After 600yds (549m) reach signpost at Point **❸**. Keep ahead and retrace outward route to Point **❷**. Turn **L** on tarred lane, which becomes track. At Kinloch house bear **R**, then turn **L** through kissing gate, with 2nd beyond leading into plantation with signpost for Strathpeffer.
❽ Follow main path ahead until you see Strathpeffer on **R**. At next junction bear **R** down wood edge and turn **R** into town. Street on **L** leads past church with square steeple, where you turn **R** to main square.

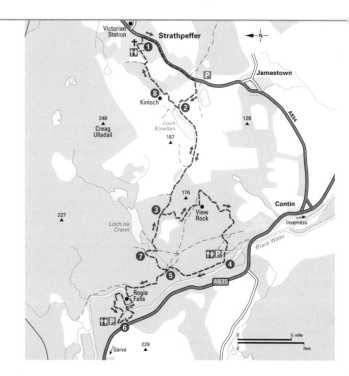

MAINLAND ORKNEY The Gloup Loop
An easy walk with an abundance of wildlife.

4 miles/6.4km 2hrs 30min **Ascent** 93ft/28m ▲ **Difficulty** ☐1
Paths Continuous, 6 kissing gates
Map OS Explorer 461 Orkney – East Mainland **Grid ref** HY 590079
Parking Mull Head car park

❶ Leave car park at **R-H** corner, where there is information plaque. Follow direction sign along gravel path to The Gloup, and 2 viewing platforms.
❷ Past The Gloup you see red-painted kissing gate and directional sign pointing **L**; this leads along grassy footpath to Brough of Deerness (pronounced broch), but more interesting route, perhaps, is straight ahead and then **L** along cliff edge, also following grassy path.
❸ At Brough is another information plaque and, in cliff edge, precipitous stone staircase which takes you down cliff and, by turning **R** at the beach, into a sheltered stony bay, Little Burra Geo. You will see, in edge of Brough wall, steep dirt path which you can climb with help of chain set into rock. Path will take you to top of Brough so that you can explore ancient site here.
❹ Having climbed back to main route, another red-painted kissing gate on **R** shows footpath leading along to cairn at Mull Head. From cairn path turns **L** and becomes much narrower, although still clear,

taking you along northern cliff edge.
❺ Path turns sharp **L** just before wire fence and climbs uphill through moorland to another red-painted kissing gate.
❻ Turn **R** here and go down to red kissing gate you see in fencing above farmhouse, East Denwick. Here turn **L** along wide hill track. Just above farmhouse, pass through another red kissing gate and track becomes very overgrown. At top **L** turn leads downhill to red kissing gate on **L**.
❼ Narrow grass path through gate and between wire fences turns sharp **R** and leads back into car park.

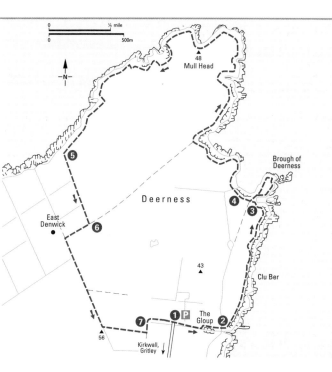

Walking in Safety

All these walks are suitable for any reasonably fit person, but less experienced walkers should try the easier walks first. Route finding is usually straightforward, but you will find that an Ordnance Survey map is a vital addition to the route maps and descriptions.

Risks

Although each walk has been researched with a view to minimising the risks to the walkers who follow its route, no walk in the countryside can be considered to be completely free from risk. Walking in the outdoors will always require a degree of common sense and judgement to ensure that it is as safe as possible.

- Be particularly careful on cliff paths and in upland terrain, where the consequences of a slip can be very serious.

- Remember to check tidal conditions before walking along the seashore.

- Some sections of route are by, or cross roads. Take care and remember traffic is a danger even on minor country lanes.

- Be careful around farmyard machinery and livestock, especially if you have children or a dog with you.

- Be aware of the consequences of changes of weather and check the forecast before you set off. Carry spare clothing and a torch if you are walking in the winter months. Remember that the weather can change very quickly at any time of the year, and in moorland and heathland areas, mist and fog can make route finding much harder. Don't set out in these conditions unless you are confident of your navigation skills in poor visibility. In summer remember to take account of the heat and sun; wear a hat and carry spare water.

- On walks away from centres of population you should carry a whistle and survival bag. If you do have an accident requiring the emergency services, make a note of your position as accurately as possible and dial 999.